Praise for Cyndy Etler's *The Dead Inside*

"Raw and absorbing, Etler's voice captivates."

—*Kirkus Reviews*

"An unnerving and heartrending memoir...readers may be stunned that a place like Straight could exist, let alone that a parent would willingly send a child there."

—*Publishers Weekly*

"Etler weaves her story with conviction, self-deprecating humor, and hard facts... Readers will come to respect the fighter that Etler is and the advocate she became for other teens in similar situations."

—*Booklist*

"You don't so much read [this memoir] as you watch, through a dark and hazy window, as a child's soul is destroyed. A must-read for parents, teachers, counselors, and students."

—Mercy Pilkington, 2010 National Juvenile
Detention Association Teacher of the Year

"Prepare yourself. On page one, a young Etler takes your hand and she doesn't let go. Though condemned to sixteen months of darkness—figurative and literal—Etler shines light on the controversial treatment

D0763287

You won't be able to put [this book] down, and you sure as hell won't root this hard for anyone else ever again."

—Rosella Eleanor LaFevre, Editor-in-Chief,

M.L.T.S. Magazine

"We, the survivors of Straight, wish we could make you understand what it was like. That we could put you in our skin, take you back in time, and sit you down in group. So you could...feel the loss of yourself. Etler honors the many of us who still can't talk about it, and the many that were unable to survive. Somehow, Etler tells her story without making it about her."

—Marcus Chatfield, coproducer, *Surviving Straight Inc.: The Documentary*

WE
CAN'T BE
FRIENDS

ALSO BY CYNDY ETLER

The Dead Inside

WE
CAN'T BE
FRIENDS

A TRUE STORY

cyndy etler

sourcebooks
fire

Published by Sourcebooks Fire, an imprint of Sourcebooks, Inc.
P.O. Box 4410, Naperville, Illinois 60567-4410
(630) 961-3900
Fax: (630) 961-2168
sourcebooks.com

Library of Congress Cataloging-in-Publication Data

Names: Etler, Cyndy, author.
Title: We can't be friends / Cyndy Etler.
Description: Naperville, Illinois : Sourcebooks Fire, [2017]
Identifiers: LCCN 2017013495 | (hardcover : alk. paper)
Subjects: LCSH: Drug addicts--Rehabilitation--United States--Juvenile
    literature. | Problem youth--United States--Juvenile literature. | High
    school girls--United States--Juvenile literature.
Classification: LCC HV5825 .E843 2017 | DDC 363.2092 [B] --dc23 LC record
available at https://lccn.loc.gov/2017013495

Printed and bound in the United States of America.
MA 10 9 8 7 6 5 4 3 2 1

This book's for you, Rich. You carried that weight a long time. Through the darkness you couldn't see it, but you were everyone's light.

High school sucks for a lot of people. High school extra-sucks when you believe, deep in your soul, that every kid in school is out to get you.

I wasn't popular before I got locked up in Straight, Inc., the notorious "tough love" program for troubled teens. So it's not like I was walking around thinking everyone liked me. But when you're trapped in a warehouse for sixteen months with no distractions—no books or friends or TV; no stepping outside; no *school*, even—your mind gets a little crazy. When you're psychologically beaten for six-teen months, you start to absorb the lessons. The lessons in Straight were: You are evil. Your peers are evil. Everything is evil except Straight, Inc.

Before long, you're a true believer.

When you're finally released and sent back out into the world—to your high school full of evil peers and dangerous influences—you need to be back where it's safe. To be back in the warehouse. And if you can't be there, you'd rather be dead.

This is the story of my return to my high school. This is the story of the kids there who seemed evil, and the adults who seemed nice. This is the true story of how I didn't die.

I'm sitting on the roof next to Doug Bianchi. Yes, *that* Doug Bianchi. Short little muscle guy. Popular kid. His Rabbit is in the driveway with the windows down. I can smell his stack of pine tree air fresheners from here. Doug's car is the only one parked right, with four wheels on pavement and the emergency brake pulled up. His best friend, Brent Riga, left his Rabbit on the street at a "hit me, I dare ya" angle. Zack Fox's Jeep has two wheels in his house's front flower bed. Ty Norse's Jeep is the bull's-eye in the middle of Zack's front lawn.

I am at a two-Jeep party. *Me.* I'm on the roof of the pool house in Zack's side yard, looking down at the cool guys' parking jobs. Their cars graph out the social order. Doug gives too much of a fuck—seventeen air fresheners—and Zack gives zero.

cyndy etler

I couldn't find this place again if I tried. It's on one of those tiny fake streets Monroe's founding fathers penciled onto the map just to fuck with us. There're two houses, three, tops. There's not even a street sign. But Doug got here lickety-split, like a homing pigeon. Doug *belongs*.

When we first got here, Doug checked his alignment in the rearview mirror, grabbed the six-pack I didn't know was behind my seat, pushed his door open, and said, "Stay here." Then he walked in Zack's front door, no doorbell, no knock. Doug belongs like *that*.

For a while I'm the only girl at a two-Jeep party, which probably makes you wonder, "Where are the parents?!" But that's because you don't know Zack Fox. He's not a kid like us. He's from frigging Canada, for one thing. His two front teeth are removable, from a hockey incident. His eyes are green and his hair covers one of them and he drives a Jeep. Kids like Zack? They don't have parents or bowel movements or weird shit from their past they don't talk about. They just *are*, and they're perfect.

Zack is sitting up on the roof with us, on the other side of Doug. He's one Doug away from me, with his tan bare feet and his fray-bottomed Levi's. He's so cool even popular Doug, in his purple-flowered Jams, looks like a clown next to him. Doug sounds like a clown too. He's talking wicked fast about some rude thing his brother did and how he's gonna join the marines and show his brother, who's only in the navy.

"Shadd*AP*, Dougie," yells Ty.

I can't believe Ty talked. Legends don't talk. They do shit like float around the pool in a Styrofoam armchair, with their eyes closed and their paw gripping an uncracked beer. Doug, the un-legend, keeps yammering.

"Jeezus, kid. What're you, on coke?" Ty yells, which makes Zack laugh, and Brent laugh, and Doug turn bright, bright red. I kinda laugh too, even though I'm not supposed to. I mean, I came here with Doug. Without him, I wouldn't be within a trillion miles of this place.

Doug gets me back though, when the pink Buick pulls up with the popular girls. Wendi Rosini gets out and looks up at me, first thing.

"Cyndy *Etler*?" she says, hard, and Doug just shrugs.

Kathy Radcliff gets out of the driver's side, and Tiffani Malta gets out of the back. They start talking in voices I can't hear. I get really interested in the roof tiles.

"I'm going in*side*, Zack," Wendi says. This time Zack shrugs.

"Okay *thanks*, Wendi," Brent says back to her, and cannonballs off the diving board onto Ty.

I'm here. At a popular party. Laughing at a joke about cocaine. If the people at Straight could see me now, I'd be on the firing line. Three hundred ex-druggies would be gearing up to spit on me, screeching, *Sobriety! Slippery slope!*

You'd have to live it to understand. Straight doesn't give

a single fuck if nobody likes you, if the whole school stops talking and stares when you walk in the room. Straight doesn't care if being at a real, live, popular kid's party is the moment you've been waiting for your whole life. Straight only cares about one thing: your piece-of-shit druggie ass staying sober. And I am the ultimate Straightling. At least, I was for the sixteen months I spent in Straight. And when I first got out, three years ago. But…now I'm here. I rode in a car with a six-pack of beer. And I laughed at a cocaine joke.

Wendi, of course, is Zack's girlfriend. You've never seen anyone shine so hard. She's got muscle legs *and* her cut-offs are an un-tight size eight. In all the years we've had classes together, I've talked to her once—that day we had English outside and I was feeling really good about myself. As she walked back inside ahead of me, I said, "I love your hair. Where do you get it done?" and she just said, "Thanks" with, like, her sneeze face on. As if saying that one syllable was so painful.

Doug has stopped talking now, and Zack never talks, and of course, I'm not saying a frigging word. We're all in some mystical land in our heads, picturing how Wendi is gonna look in her, no doubt, fucking string bikini.

I hear the crack of the opening can at the same second Brent starts yelling. It sounds like the crack of a—

"Doug! Douggieee! Jump, Dougie! Jump!"

He's splashing in the shallow end, curling his arms, to

show Doug the path from roof to pool. There's another crack, and Zack passes Doug one of the beers he must have had in his Levi's back pockets. That's twice today that beer has been within three feet of me. And I laughed at a cocaine joke. Who the fuck *am* I?

"Dougie baby! Come to mama!" goes Brent.

The popular girls cross the driveway in little tank tops with their bikini straps showing. They're gonna take off their tops and be all laughy and beautiful. And Doug's gonna jump off this roof into the pool. And Ty and Brent are gonna fuck around trying to drown each other, and Zack will be silent and golden, surveying his domain. And I'll be the clean and sober black hole, all covered up in mom shorts and sneakers. I'll be tongue-tied and quivering—*slippery slope!*—because somebody smells like a beer. *Cyndy Etlerrr.*

"Here," Doug says, shoving his—his *beer* into my hand.

I hold it by two fingers like it burns. "Wait, I—"

"Go ahead," Doug says. "Take a sip."

"Do it, Cyn," Zack says.

"Douggieee!" Brent yells.

"Doug-ie! Doug-ie!" says Ty, Brent, and those girls, muffled by the tank tops they're pulling over their heads. "Doug-ie! Doug-ie!"

"You take a sip, and I jump," Doug says to me.

My stomach dips like *I* jumped off the roof because *SOBRIETY!*

The elite-level popular kids are all watching.

"One sip," Doug says. "I jump. Ready, set, *go*."

FOUR YEARS AND SEVEN
MONTHS EARLIER

NOVEMBER 1985

Straight Warehouse, Intake Room
FIRST DAY IN

"No, you don't get it. I don't need frigging rehab!" I say. "I only tried pot. *Tried*. Like, three times." I'm looking at his badge. It says STAFF.

"That's the insanity of your disease, Cyndy. You believe you have control over your drug use." STAFF guy's voice is a flat monotone. "If you had control over your drug use, your parents wouldn't have brought you to an intensive drug treatment program like Straight, Inc." He's a robot repeating a memorized script.

"But I don't even know *how* to smoke pot. I've never even *seen* another drug!"

"That's called denial. Mark that on her intake form."

Group Room, Facing Hundreds of Straightlings
TWO DAYS IN

"I'm sorry, but I'm not like you all," I say to the hundreds of them. "I don't *do* drugs. I only tried smoking pot a couple times. I'm—"

"Dry druggie! You're a dry druggie!" It's a girl, screaming at me. "You belong here *just* as much as I do, as we *all* do! You're going to sit in that blue chair and *rot* until you admit it!"

Open Meeting: Hundreds of Parents & Straightlings
TWO DAYS IN

STAFF guy picks up the microphone. "Where are the parents who signed their kids into Straight this week? Will all of you please stand up?"

APPLAUSE

"You are brave, moms and dads. Very brave. You signed your child into Straight, Inc., knowing you won't see him or her for a good long time. You proved your commitment to your child's sobriety by writing that first check."

My mother stands across the warehouse from me. She's one of twelve, smiling like the applause is hers, all hers. Her eyes are on STAFF, hungry. Some of the other moms scan the group of Straightlings—hundreds of oldcomers, who've been here forever, plus us twelve newcomers, who've been here a day or two—looking for their kids. But not my mother. She's not looking for me.

"And you are wise, moms and dads. You know that, underneath all of the pain your kid caused you, underneath all that druggie behavior, there's a life-threatening disease. Whether your child is just getting started on their druggie career or is knee deep in it, you know that, without Straight, he or she would be dead, and soon. You are such a loving parent, you will sacrifice everything to save your child's life."

APPLAUSE

"Welcome to your new life, moms and dads," STAFF guy tells them. "We love you."

My mother looks at the parents sitting around her. She wants a hug, to start her new life.

"Now, Straightlings," STAFF guy snaps. "Let's have a song! How about 'We Love You Straight'?"

The hundreds of zombies lurch into song.

We love you Straight

Oh, yes we do

We love you Straight

And we'll be true…

I sit and move my lips in the shape of, "Mom. Please. Mom."

Group Room
THREE DAYS IN

My mother is gone. Home. She's three hundred miles away, sipping herbal tea.

I'm standing in front of the Straightlings. A cute boy is spitting on me.

"You think this group is buying your act, Cyndy? Little Miss Priss? 'Wah! I've only smoked pot! I'm a virgin! My daddy hit me! Poor me!' *Bull*shit! You're a druggie whore, like every other girl in this group. You leave here, you'll be dead or in jail within a month. Quit whining and face your reality. You're here! You're an addict! Deal with it!"

U.S. Route 50, Dodge Minivan with My Oldcomer, Her Mother, and Her Father
FOUR DAYS IN

I'm staring at the Caravan's digital clock. It's 10:17 p.m. My oldcomer's finger started jabbing toward my breastbone at 10:14. It made contact at 10:15.

"You better get honest with the group, Little Cyndy Cries-a-Lot. You better admit to your addiction. You see me? I'm nineteen years old. I don't have to be here. I *choose* to be at Straight because Straight saved my life. I got signed in when I was seventeen, when I'd 'only smoked pot and drank beer.' Sound familiar? I didn't have a drug problem. No way! Day I turned eighteen? I signed myself out. Three days later I was snorting coke off the floor of a truck stop men's room. I fucked a guy as old as my father to get it. Doesn't that sound fun? That's your *future*, little Cyndy, if you don't admit to your addiction. You need to thank God that your parents found Straight before your druggie ass found cocaine."

"Amen," her mother says from the front seat. Her father hits the blinker and smooths into the fast lane.

We left the Straight building at 9:30 p.m. We'll get to her house at 11:30. We'll lie on a mattress from midnight to 6:00. We'll leave for the building again at 6:30.

Group Room
FIVE DAYS IN

"Cyndy Etlerrr! Where are you? Stand your ass up!" STAFF guy yells at the hundreds of us. "Cyndy *still* hasn't gotten honest about her drug list, group! Day five, and she's *still* singing the 'Poor me, I only tried pot' song. Can you believe it?"

I don't think I have a mother anymore. I'm not sure I ever had a mother.

"Cyndy's got some *balls!*" STAFF guy yells. "Who's got something to say to Cyndy? Who wants to give wittle baby Cyndy some spit therapy?"

RAHHHRRRRR!

Group Room
SIX DAYS IN

I shake my hands in the air to get called on. I stand up. They stare at me.

7

"I—I want—I want to get honest, about the drugs I've done? Um, I smoked pot once in September, and again in October, but I heard somebody say something about hash one time, so maybe there was hash in the pot? Or like, hash…oil? So I've done pot, and hash, and hash oil…and one time I tried to kill myself by taking a bottle of aspirin, so I've also done over-the-counter drugs…and I did drink beer once, so I've done alcohol…"

"Good *job*, Cyndy!" STAFF says. "Group, are we proud of Cyndy? Tell Cyndy you love her!"

"*Love ya, Cyndy!*" they all say. The *hundreds*.

Group Room
EIGHT DAYS IN

STAFF stands me up in group.

"Say it, Cyndy. Say the words: 'I am a drug addict.'"

"But I—I only—"

"You! Are! An! Addict! If you don't admit it and accept Straight's help, you're going to die. In a gutter. With a needle jammed in your arm. You'll be sucking Satan's cock in a ditch somewhere! Say the words!"

"I—I—"

"Group, who wants to—"

RAHHHRRRRR!

Open Meeting: Hundreds of Parents and Straightlings
TEN DAYS IN

The mother is across the warehouse from me. This time, she stands up alone.

"You have to hold the mic right up to your mouth, Mom," STAFF says. "Try again."

"Cyndy? I—"

"*MOM!*" I say, without even realizing.

"*SHHHHHHHH!*" the hundreds say back to me.

The mother is talking into the mic. "The staff told me you won't admit to your addiction, Cyndy. So I have to use my tough love to help you. I am not going to sign you out of the program. Ever. You can either work this program and graduate, or you can sit in that blue plastic chair until you turn eighteen."

Ten days ago, when she left me here, I was fourteen. Six weeks before that, when I ran away from her house and her husband, I was thirteen.

She's still going. "But if you sign yourself out? When you turn eighteen? Do not call me. Do not come to my house. You either admit to your addiction and work this program or you are dead to me. I love you, Cyndy."

Today, I am ageless. I am dust. I am nothing.

Group Room
ELEVEN DAYS IN

"I'd like to get honest with the group? I'm Cyndy, and I *do* believe I'm a drug addict. The drugs I've done are pot, alcohol, hash, hash oil, and T-Thai weed? And over-the-counter drugs."

"LOOOOOVE YA, CYNDY!"

Group Room
TWO MONTHS IN

There's a new girl three inches in front of me.

"You need to quit feeling sorry for yourself and get honest!" I yell at her face. "I don't care that you're only fifteen. I'm only fourteen! And I had the *exact* same pity party for myself when I got here."

The fluorescent bulbs make my spittle, on her cheekbones, sparkle and glint.

"'Wittle Baby Cyndy' was my name, because I refused to face my addiction, just like you! What drugs have you really done? Spill it!"

Yesterday, she was fifteen. Today, she's ageless. She's dust. She's nothing.

Group Room
SEVEN MONTHS IN

We're all in a great mood because Mitch, everybody's favorite, is tonight's staff.

"Group, listen up!" Mitch yells. "Our friend Chris here turned eighteen today, and guess *what*? He put in for a withdrawal! Chris is ready to go out there and live drug free on his own! He doesn't need you anymore, group. Who wants to say goodbye before he signs himself out?"

RAHHHRRRRR!

"Andrey!" Mitch says, pointing at a kid on the guy's side. "You're Chris's host brother, right? Chris has been sleeping at your house, eating your parents' food, for how many months? Give Chris a hug! Tell him you'll miss—"

"YOU are going to DIE," Andrey howls, jumping up and racing at Chris like a bullet. "To DIE, motherfucker. You need this fucking group to stay sober and alive! You go out there, you're going to pick up the first beer you see! And that one beer? An addict like you? You'll be dead in a week! Freedom is a slippery slope, bro. Have a good fucking funeral."

"*Love ya, Andrey!*" we all scream as he sits back down. "*Bye, Chris!*"

Group Room
EIGHT MONTHS IN

"*Group!* Put your hands down! Eyes up here!"

12

We do it, lightning quick. We've never heard Mitch sound pissed before.

"You all are *fucked*. I am so scared for this group because you don't give a *shit* about your sobriety and you don't give a *shit* about each other."

Mitch's face is as red as his hair.

"Who remembers Chris? Chris, who signed himself out the second he turned eighteen because you fuckups didn't hold him accountable? Who you let get away with self-pity and 'I've got this' fantasies? Chris is fucking *dead*. He fucking hung himself. Who wants to die at eighteen like Chris? Go ahead! I'll throw the doors open! Seriously! Which of you fucking druggies wants to leave now?"

We sit here, still as stones. None of us are breathing. Mitch is breathing fire.

"You fuckups don't know because we keep you safe and secure in this building twelve hours a day, but us staff, we hear it all the time: Straightlings fucking killing themselves. Did you know that? They go back out there, and they realize how fucked they are, and sayonara. Adios. G'bye. I could give you three more names of kids you know just from the past six months! It is *deadly* out there. You ungrateful pussies need to work your *asses* off to get fucking sober and to get each *other* sober. No, put your hands down. I don't want to hear your *feelings*. Let's have a fucking song. 'Fire and Rain.'"

We try to sing because Mitch said to. We can hear the click of tears in each other's voices.

March 1987

Open Meeting: Hundreds of Parents and Straightlings
SIXTEEN MONTHS, ONE WEEK, AND TWO DAYS IN

"Parents, group, it's a big night," Mitch booms into the mic. "I need the following Straightlings to come stand at the front with me: Eva Black, Steve Kettle, Deidre Smith, Rob Robinson, Sal Oak, and Cyndy Etler. Parents of newcomers, I want you to take a good look at these clear-eyed, iron-spined young people, because they represent your child's future."

We six Straightlings stand military-still in the space between the group and the parents. We're lined up like slaves on an auction block. Mitch looks each of us in the eye, then looks back at the throng of parents.

"The commitment you made this week, newcomer parents? To trust Straight, to sacrifice, to make any necessary investment of time and money? That commitment will pay off the day your druggie kid is standing here, ready to graduate: honest, loving, and drug free. On that day, we will proudly hand your child back to you, to go out into the world and thrive. To carry Straight's message to other druggies. And, by the grace of God, to remain Straight. Congratulations,

Eva, Steve, Deidre, Rob, Sal, and Cyndy. You are now, officially, graduates of Straight, Inc."

The mass of parents, the hundreds of Straightlings, they roar and clap and whistle. But we six, suddenly freed—we're in a standing coma. We have clenched jaws and fists and hearts and bowels. Freedom is a slippery slope.

Still March 1987

Masuk High School, Principal's Office
THREE DAYS OUT

"We're so glad you're returning to Masuk, Cyndy. Do you know how special you are? You are our only clean and sober student. You're going to be a powerful influence on the student body! If you will excuse me for just a moment, I'll get your file."

CLICK.

"Mom, I've got to pee."

"So go pee."

"No, you have to take me! I'm not allowed to go to the bathroom by myself!"

"Cyndy, that's enough of that. You're *out* of the program. There are no more *rules*."

"B-but—but this is my druggie high school! My druggie *friends* are out there! I—I can't—"

"Now you listen to me: we are *done* with that. Don't bother me with any more of your rules and permissions!"

"But I'll die! I'll be using in a week! I'll be in a ditch, sucking the devil's cock! I'll—"

SLAP.

"Cynthia. Drew. Etler. Stop this. Now. I've done my part. I put you through Straight. Now go to the bathroom or wet your pants. It's your choice."

CLICK.

"Okay then, Mom, Cyndy! Thanks for being patient. Here's your reenrollment paperwork. Mom, if you'll sign here, we can get Cyndy's schedule made up. She can start back at Masuk bright and early tomorrow morning. We're so glad to have you back, Cyndy."

I can't believe I don't get in trouble. I mean, every single *day*, I walk in late. Just, whenever I get here. And nobody says a word.

At Straight, I would get slaughtered for this. But at Straight, I had oldcomers and host sisters to force me up from the safe, sweet coffin of sleep. Now, it's just me. I let myself stay dead a lot longer.

When I finally get here, I come in that side door nobody ever uses and follow the silent, empty hallway to math class. If a teacher has her door open, the classroom full of faces turns and drop-jaw stares at me. Fuck 'em, though. I lift my giant Dunkin' Donuts mug at them, like, *Top o' the morning, suckers.*

That's what makes Blanca Halliwell talk to me—my Dunkin' Donuts mug. You would want to talk to me about it too. You've never seen anything like it. Picture a beehive, with those puffy bump-lines wrapped all around it. Now chop the hive in half and stick a handle on it, plus a faded orange "Dunkin'" and a faded pink "Donuts." That's my mug. You can fit a half a coffeepot in there, which I do, every day.

Still. Blanca Halliwell? She's got the prettiest hair in all of Masuk: long and blond and curly. She's a cheerleader, she never smiles, *and* she drives a Jetta. Does she not *know* about me?

I sit behind her in social studies, which is the boringest class ever. So she kills the boredom one day by spinning backward and grabbing my mug. It's as if she can't see the inch-thick cube of Plexiglas, plus barbed wire, plus the flashing, red sign that says *STAY BACK!* surrounding me.

"You're always carrying this," she says, laughing. "What do you *have* in here? Vodka?" Then she brings it to her nose and smells it.

I've been out of Straight a couple months now, so I don't totally flip. But if she'd asked me if I drank vodka when I was still in the program? Oh my *God*. They woulda carried me out of that room in a straightjacket. I guess I've gotten a teeny bit chill since then, 'cause I just say, "No, it's coffee. My latest addiction." And she laughs at me. Or *with* me, I guess. Which is a huge difference.

Thank God she turns forward then, 'cause what the hell

else can I say? I'm an addict. That's all I got. But when I tell you it's a miracle that Blanca Halliwell talked to me, believe me: it is a *miracle*. Nobody talks to me. Except the teachers. Which somehow underlines the fact that nobody else does.

You know what makes it even worse? When I first got back from Straight, the cool kids tried to talk to me. The cool kids who were my *druggie friends* back when I was drinking and drugging. Or at least, when I would have been drinking and drugging, if I'd been able to get alcohol or drugs. My first *day* back at Masuk, my best friend Joanna came right up to me! It was like the sun rising after some horrible midnight earthquake: the best and the worst thing that could happen all at once. I stutter-stepped away from her, head tucked in my armpit, then hid in the bathroom for two hours, trying to scrub the shit off my undies.

Joanna is *every*thing, but she's also the most dangerous thing. For thirteen years, before I met her, I never had an actual friend. Then I had Joanna. For three whole months! Then I got put in Straight and learned she was a bad influence. A druggie friend. And now, I'm back to having zero friends. Actually *extra* zero because I'm the freak who disappeared one day, then came back a year and a half later as a program zombie. People can't wait to not be friends with me.

Truth, though? I want Jo back as my friend. More than *any*thing. But if Straight heard me say that, I'd get creamed. I'd get slapped back in there so fast, our heads would spin.

So yeah. When you've been locked in a warehouse for sixteen months of tough love therapy, converting back to the real world is hard. School is this daily Roman gladiator match: druggie friends on one side, nosy teachers who want to "help" on the other. I'm in the middle, holding my Dunkin' mug like a shield, as the Blancas and Brents and Kathys, the eagle-eyed popular kids, watch from the sidelines. As the dungeon of Straight, Inc., looms in the background, waiting for me to screw up. Could you blame me for daydreaming suicide?

Suicide doesn't run in my "family," if you can call it that. Crazy does. And mean. But not suicide. The people with my DNA, they keep on living. Living and bitching about it.

Except my father. He ducked out early, but that wasn't suicide. It was more like popularity. People—my mother, his ex-wives, his students, his kids, his fans—they loved him so much, they crushed him. He crawled into a hospital one day, a year after I was born, and dropped dead. Doctor said maybe it was pneumonia. I know better. He was too bright a star for this world. He just couldn't last here.

I wonder what he'd think if he could see how his last wife—my mother—and his kids are living now, in the big, rotting house my mother and her second husband, Jacque, found when she got pregnant again. The one with all these bedrooms for her kids + his kids + their kid. The one with enough space for everybody's secrets.

It feels like, when they sent me to Straight, the hole I left became a vortex. All the secrets got sucked into it, and my mother couldn't ignore them. I'm just guessing, though. I wasn't here to see it. But now, eighteen months after she sent me away, the only people left in the house are my mother and my baby half sister. And me, of course. But I disappear so much, I barely count.

Believe me, you wouldn't pull up a chair in this place, either. Every surface is sticky with old food, mother junk, and sickening memories. I **SHOOSH** along the path I've made from the front door to the coffeemaker to the cracker cabinet to my room. Occasional field trip to the bathroom, but only when my mother is at work. Your goal would be the same as mine: Don't. Get. Seen.

My mother is like handcuffs. If she sees you, don't even try to run. Don't touch anything. Just put your hands in your pockets, put on your pity face, and nod. When she pauses, go, "Oh, that sucks for you, poor thing." She'll stop, eventually. Give it an hour. And know, *know*, you'll be staying with my baby sister for all of next Saturday. Unpaid.

She's gonna bitch about *every*thing. Her support group, Al-Anon, taught her about how her life is full of alkies: her father, her husband Jacque, me… And how we've all been so cruel to her, even though she's tried and tried to please us. She'll tear up when she tells you about Her Alvin, my father. How he was the only one who ever loved her, and how she only had him for seven years. She'll perk back up, though, when she gets to Straight. Straight, Inc.! Straight *saved* her by introducing her to Al-Anon, by showing her how her alcoholic, druggie daughter was ruining her life!

Go ahead. Ask me how I could possibly be an alcoholic and drug addict when I only drank once and smoked pot twice. I see that raised brow. You just don't get it. You don't know what a dry druggie is. But I'll clue you in. A dry druggie is someone who has the Disease—alcoholism and addiction—even if they haven't started using yet. Just because the substance isn't in the person, that doesn't mean the disease isn't. You know that saying, "if it quacks like a duck"? Well, how about "if it acts like a druggie"? Yeah. Straight taught me plenty too.

When my mother's done crying, she'll go up to her bed and snuggle with her Al-Anon flyers. She's got a thousand of them, all over her bed and nightstand. She's also got five Hazelden "recovery meditation" books: *Daily Meditations for Women Who Love Too Much*, *Daily Meditations for Women Who Work Too Much*, *Daily Meditations for Daughters of Alcoholics*, …*for Wives of Alcoholics*, …*for Mothers of Alcoholics*. They're all yellowed and thumbprint-y. They're her new blankie.

And I totally get it. Straight is *my* frigging blankie. Okay, it was hell until I accepted my addiction. But now? Like, if I could go back and be on staff? I'd do it in a millisecond. I'd staple myself to the back wall in a sleeping bag and only come out to lead discussion groups. Oh my God, can you imagine how *safe* life would be? Living where everyone gets you? It would be the opposite of this plague, slunking through Masuk and chipping away the hours in this house.

The only reason I can sort of deal is because Jacque is gone. In my mother's great flash of awareness, she realized that Jacque's not good for her, so she's divorcing him. Thank you, Jesus *God*. When I was in Straight, I had to tell him— *gah*. We all had to say "I love you" to our parents, which meant I had to say it to my mother's husband. And I had to apologize for making him do things to me. Because everything was my fault, so I had been, like, acting flirty when I was a four-year-old, I guess. Which made him...

Anyway.

If I had to *live* with him after that? Nuh-uh. I would've fucked up my sobriety so quick, they'd have overnight expressed me back to Straight. I wouldn't even care how hellish it was, starting the program over. I just would *not* live with him again. But I don't have to worry about that, because he's gone.

There *is* something great in my life, though: my recovery meetings. They're what I live for. I started out going to the Alcoholics Anonymous meetings in Trumbull, the next town over. And I still go to them, because it's all older people who feel like substitute parents. But I've discovered a whole other world of meetings too. Meetings you would not *believe*.

Down in the rich towns, like Fairfield and Westport, they mainly have CoDa meetings—Codependents Anonymous. They're my favorite because they're held in this triangular side hall at a big, modern church that's all windows with views of pine trees. The people at CoDa, they're different. They talk about actual life, their jobs and friendships, instead of only saying, "It works if you work it" and "One day at a time." A lot of them do art or music, and they wear scarves and boots and purple. And they drive cool cars! For example, this one guy—he looks *exactly* like Molly Ringwald's boyfriend in *Sixteen Candles*, with even the werewolf *V* of hair on his forehead—drives a Porsche. And this other lady, who smiles so much you think she'll *tee-hee!* like the Pillsbury Doughboy if you push her tummy, drives a beat-up Jeep. She's got a Martha Washington hairdo and skirts to her ankles, and she drives a topless Jeep. I frigging *love* CoDa. It's like hanging out with the cool kids.

Then, totally different, are the meetings in Bridgeport. They've got NA, Narcotics Anonymous, and CA, Cocaine Anonymous. Those meetings are held in fluorescent-bulb-lit hospital rooms, which is kind of a weird place to be. Somehow the guy sitting next to me—it's always a guy—is wearing a plastic garbage bag for a raincoat. Or a seafoam hospital dress and paper shoes.

At CA and NA, they don't talk about art or serenity. They talk about drugs. Drugs like pollution, like a river on fire. When I sit in a CA meeting and hear about their drugs, I'm like, *Damn.* The drugs us Straightlings did were dipped in rainbow sprinkles. Nobody at Straight talked about the smell of the shit they hacked up on their concrete bed, like these guys. Nobody mentioned the DTs or buggy face scabs or pulling the trigger of a loaded gun to kill the feeling of coming down. Holy crap, Bridgeport.

So yeah. It can get pretty creepy, sitting in a tidy row of Masuk desks, sunbeams streaming down on me and the rest of the deodorized fifteen-year-olds. It's just too...civilized. I'm more comfortable holding hands with dirt-nailed junkies for the closing NA prayer. The junkies, they don't have curly blond hair that's way prettier than mine. Plus, you can tell they mean it when they say, "Nice fucking Dunkin' mug you got there."

Most meetings in my AA booklet have a secret code next to them, like *NC* or *O* or *BB*. The code tells you what the meeting will be like. *NC* means it's for newcomers. *O* means it's an open meeting, so you could bring your nonaddict friends, if you had any. *BB* means they talk about the Big Book of Alcoholics Anonymous, which is totally *yawn*. Only like every fiftieth meeting has *my* secret code, *YP*. My heart's still stupid enough to trampoline when it sees *YP*, but my brain isn't. There are no real "young people" in recovery. I'm the only freak. The next youngest are like in their twenties.

That's okay though. People in their twenties have cars, which they'll sometimes use to pick me up for the cool meetings. I would *love* to have actual teenagers to talk to about sobriety and making amends and stuff, but that's almost greedy. I have my *sobriety*. That's God's greatest gift. And I'm gonna tell Him that He needs to give me more? That's disgusting. That makes me want to slap my face.

It's actually really rare that any of the meeting people in their twenties come out to Monroe to pick me up. Because then they'd have to drive me back too. A single meeting could turn into a six-hour field trip. So mostly I live at the Trumbull meetings, because AA grownups will totally come get me.

But I signed up for driver's ed, which means someday, I'll have a license! Which means I can blackmail my mother into letting me use her car! Seriously. This free-babysitting-Saturday situation is out of control. But what am I gonna say? It's not like I have anywhere else I've gotta be. When I can drive, though? Then I'll have places to be. I'll hang out with the cool Westport meeting people. I'll go back and hang out at Straight.

If you're a Straight graduate who lives in the same city as a Straight building, you get to still hang out there. If you're on a slippery slope and your sobriety's at risk, you can just go be with all the Straightlings. And since all the Straights are in actual cities, if you live near one, you've got frigging cable TV and probably a subway to take you to meetings. I've got three staticky channels, a sister in diapers, and a five-mile walk to the closest store. I can't even call any Straightlings because we can't afford long distance.

When I have my license, though, I'll be able to say to my

mother, "You let me use your car tonight or I won't babysit Saturday." She'll be forced to say yes, because she *needs* me to stay with my baby sister. Because she *lives* for going out with her boyfriends. You should see her all fired up, singing and putting on that blue mascara.

And like, me? I'm pretty into locking a bathroom door, 'cause for my first ten months at Straight, I had an oldcomer staring at me every time I used a toilet. Not my mother, though. She makes me frigging *talk* to her while she's on the pot. Her job in life is to make sure everyone is paying attention to her at all times, in all places. When she finally leaves and it's quiet, the whole house goes *ahhhh*.

––––––––

Today's Saturday. Which means (a) I'm babysitting, and (b) I'm bored out of my skull. So I'm going through the stuff on my mother's bed, where I find this book that's like, the bible of Straight, Inc. It's called *Tough Love: A Self-Help Manual for Kids in Trouble*. The cover is a picture of a heart getting crushed by a fist. This book explains everything about me and my recovery.

It starts by telling kids how to get help for their addiction, and it is *balls-out* honest, telling the reader she's a manipulative sleaze who makes people feel sorry for her, so she can keep drinking and drugging. I swear this book knew me in my past, before Straight, when I was all, "Somebody help me! My stepfather is mean!"

Then it says you have to tell your parents *exactly* what scummy stuff you've done, so you can get the help you really need. Which is exactly what we did at Straight. We told our parents about our druggie pasts in microscopic detail. So what if we hadn't done actual drugs? *Tough Love* says that stealing and lying count too. I stole candy bars from my stepsister's Halloween bag nonstop when I was little. That's 100 percent proof I'm an addict.

And when *Tough Love* talks about "group," I could swear I'm back at Straight. I can almost feel the spit land on my face. This book is the greatest discovery of my life. This book *gets* me. I need to strap it to my chest like armor before school. It's gonna help me reach my new life goal: to stop thinking I'm a victim.

My mother gave me that same feedback last week. She got home early from work, so she heard me in my bedroom, crying about…just, everything—sitting alone at lunch, having no father, knowing I could lose my sobriety any second… She rapped her knuckles on my door three times and said, "You have a really good life. I hope you know that."

It took me a while to quit hiccupping and snuffing, but when I finally shut up, I had my solution. It was so obvious even my mother could see it: I need to quit this whining and stinkin' thinkin' or no one's *ever* going to like me. God! I make myself sick.

I figured out why I never get in trouble with teachers. It's because I'm their shining hero, their dweeb among dopers. Sober Teen! They see me with, like, a cape rippling out behind me, even though I hide in the bathroom instead of going to class. Even though there's a dunce cap on my head. No wonder all the Masuk kids want to brain me.

And they don't even know how fucking pampered I am: fucking Masuk is letting me *skip my freshman year*. I missed school the whole sixteen months I was in Straight, but Masuk's like, "Never mind. Do summer school for three weeks, and we'll start you in the fall as a sophomore."

I actually *tried* to go to school when I was in Straight. Twice. When I first hit third phase, which is when you can leave the building for school or work, I moved into a host home with this doll-faced girl named Patsy. Her house was normal, but in her garage was a fucking Rolls-Royce. A *Rolls-Royce*. For exactly one day, her big, soft dad drove us to North Attleboro High School in that Rolls. That car was so smooth it was like riding a stick of butter. But that night I got assigned to a new host home, and Patsy disappeared from group.

The host home I went to next wasn't a home, exactly. It was a trailer with no wheels and a concrete building glued onto the back. Sam Lancer lived there. Sam literally scared the shit outta me my third day in, when she attacked this fat punk-rock girl in group for having a druggie hairstyle. Sam was, like, the only girl in Straight with brown skin. She was also the meanest girl there. Staff put me as her host sister so I could learn humility.

Sam and her dad were like the ≠ sign. Out of all the host dads, he was the nicest. He had gray hair and a beard he kept all perfect, like a British hedge; his face was more tan than brown. Every single night while I was Sam's host sister, I told him, "You look like Gary Gnu from *The Great Space Coaster*. 'No *gnus* is good *gnus* without Gary Gnu!'" He would laugh, and then he would go in his room and close the door all gentle, as if he was sad. And me and Sam would go to their thin metal kitchen, and she would tell me my nightly moral inventory was really lazy, and I had to redo it or else she'd report me.

I started at Sam's druggie high school, Worcester High, the day after my first night at Sam's. It was right up the street from Sam's trailer, so I got to walk back after school. Like, outside. For the twelve months it took me to get from first phase to third phase, I hadn't once been outside during daylight. How could I? For first and second phase, I was in the building from 9:00 a.m. until 9:00 p.m., or 10:00 p.m., or midnight. Even on third phase, kids aren't supposed to be outside; Straightlings are only allowed to be out of the building for school or work. So after a year of not seeing the sun, that walk from school to Sam's was a frigging miracle. I *had* to walk outside because the bus didn't run by Sam's. I had no choice but to walk, so she couldn't even report me for it. That day was the *best*.

But school itself was not the best. School was the anti-best. It was worse than swallowing fire. Seriously, *you* try walking into a giant school you've never been to before with the five zillion kids wearing Guess jeans and lightning wash and huge, florescent earrings. *You* try doing that in your humble clothes of orange high-water corduroys with no-name sneakers, and a buttoned-to-the-top brown shirt. You do that with no earrings, no makeup, and a barrette too close to your forehead. See if you don't drop your head and wing it to the guidance office, report yourself as a recovering druggie, and hide for the rest of the day. Try that, and I guarantee you'll join me and Sam in choosing work instead of school for your third phase activity. There's no *way* you'd be the only Straightling in a school full of druggies.

But work was actually killer. That concrete room on the back of Sam's trailer turned out to be Dad Lancer's business: a hair pick packaging factory. Not kidding. There were a trillion hair picks—five different sizes, twelve different colors—and stacks of flattened black-and-yellow display boxes. Our job was to fit the right size picks in the right size display box, then run the box through the shrink wrap machine. It was like packaging rainbows.

We played the Top 40 station and made up sober lyrics—the singer would be like *…and drink some cherry wine, uh-huh!* but we were all *…and drink some cherry COKE, uh-huh!*

It was *so* fun. We danced around and stacked rainbows, and Sam forgot that she was mean and I was soft. As soon as we crossed through the doorway back into her trailer, Sam had to put back on her horns and tail and become a Straightling again. But for those eight hours every weekday, we had fun.

So yeah. In sixteen months, I went to school for two days, total. And Masuk's counting that as my whole ninth grade. Because I *Just Say No to Drugs!*

Still, I have to go to Masuk every day for summer school. Mr. Littberger, the sub, is the teacher. If your name was almost identical to cheese that smells like farts, wouldn't you stay away from a career with teenagers? But he does okay. He really does. When kids yell out, "Hey, Limburger! I mean, Littberger!" he laughs right along with them. And if you go up to his desk and ask him, he'll tell you what it was like at Woodstock. He saw fucking Jimi Hendrix.

Everyone knows Mr. Littberger smokes pot. I mean, he drives a custom van. So I really shouldn't like him. And I try not to. But I can't help it. He gives kids As just for showing up. I'm not one of his disciples, dragging a chair up to his desk and camping out, but still. I can't help hearing him when he talks. And the thing he talks most about is music.

In Straight, once I got to third phase and was allowed to have music, the only safe music to listen to was Top 40. That stuff is brand-new, so it wasn't part of my druggie past. But now that I'm out, and I don't have group around to hold me accountable, I'm getting weak. I haven't slipped to the level of the Stones or Pink Floyd, but I've definitely been listening to classic rock stations. I turn it off when my druggie bands come on, but I don't have an off switch for Mr. Littberger.

Lucky for me, I *do* have a magic trick. I figured it out when Sam seven-stepped and graduated Straight while I was still on fifth phase, which meant I couldn't work at the pick factory anymore. I wanted to stay in group instead of going to school or work, but staff said I needed to develop independence. So they made me runner for the building. I had to sit in the front office all day, waiting to bring intake forms to executive staff for signatures. Which meant I was alone with my brain all day. *So* dangerous.

That's why I came up with the magic trick: I played *The Odd Couple* theme song in my head. Anytime I thought of druggie music, I smothered it with *The Odd Couple*. So now, when Mr. Littberger talks about stuff I shouldn't hear, I look out the window and mentally hit play, same as I did when I was runner.

I wonder if Mr. Littberger knows how much he's helping us kids. Even besides the second chance at better grades and the shot of hope when we finally see a 100% on our papers, he does other stuff, like playing the Grateful Dead. For some Straightlings, the Dead would be druggie ties. But not me. The Dead are like Top 40 for me; they're brand new. I wasn't cool enough to listen to them in my past.

The other day, Mr. Littberger comes in and clicks a cassette into a boom box. Then he goes, "Put your heads down. Just *listen*." And holy shit. Packaging hair picks may be like stacking rainbows, but listening to the Grateful Dead is like *swimming* in them. It's a whole playground of sound, with instruments swinging high and low, swooping and sliding around, with notes popping out like little kids on the playground shouting, "Look, Mom!" and jumping off the swing. Dead songs sound like kindergarten recess.

But the Dead aren't just a music thing; they're also a cool kid thing. No, they're *the* cool kid thing. If your shirt has a dancing bear on it or a skull with a lightning bolt through it, you have immunity from the popular kids. You're not one of them, but you don't wanna *be* one either. Which magically makes them want *you*.

Like, look at Mack. He's Masuk's one true Deadhead, with his hacky sack, his hundred Dead shirts, and his Ronald McDonald–red hair. Everybody's fine with Mack because… because he's fine with him*self*, or something. He's always smiling, he never has his homework, and he doesn't give a shit if he's eating lunch alone. So the popular kids don't make fun of him. Because he doesn't *care*.

I don't have a crush on Mack; I want to *be* Mack. But now, thanks to Mr. Littberger, I'm a teeny bit closer. I'm turned onto the Dead, which means I have the right to wear Steal Your Face, too. I can buy immunity for the price of a T-shirt.

The only question is, when summer school ends and I'm back in school-school, will the Dead be strong enough to beat the cheerleaders? Blanca can be okay, but the rest of the cheerleaders, I *totally* need protection from. Because it's not enough for them to be models straight off God's runway, in their miniature skirts and sweaters. They have to make sure the whole school knows how un-cheerleader-y I am too.

It's like my name is their favorite bubble gum. *CyndyEtlerrr*. It's always coming out of their mouth long and slow like that. But it's never when we're alone in the girls' room or something. There, they ignore me and blot their

WE CAN'T BE FRIENDS

lipstick. For *CyndyEtlerrr*, they wait until everyone's in the room, then make it the start of some horrible question. Like, "*CyndyEtlerrr*. What did *you* do Friday after the game?" This is when every single other kid in class is talking about Ty-the-legend's giant keg party.

Or, my *God*, when that one sub was taking attendance, but she couldn't read the teacher's handwriting. She goes, "Cyndy...*Hitler*?" A football player actually fell on the floor laughing, and Tiffani Malta shook her pompoms and did the ultra-*CyndyEtlerrrrrr*, extra loud. At least I swallowed my barf. So we'll see about the power of the Grateful Dead. If a Dead shirt can make the other cheerleaders talk to me like Blanca did about my Dunkin mug? I'll sell my soul to that band.

OCTOBER 1987
SEVEN MONTHS OUT

Lately, when I make it to class, the other kids laugh at me. But it almost seems friendly, because they're laughing at stuff I *say*, as if they think I'm funny. Like, take chemistry class. First of all, why am I in chemistry? Isn't there some ladder of science you have to climb to get to chemistry? Because I didn't make it up that ladder. And second, my chem teacher looks like a troll, and she hates me. But I'm trying. I look at that big grid of letters, numbers, and atoms, and I try. But my teacher whips through these complicated formulas and then, without turning around, goes, "Okay. Test on this on Friday." Then she sits down at her desk, like, *I'm done with you students.* Nobody gets it, but nobody will say anything!

So this one day, in the silence before she can pull out her chair to sit, I go, "I can't...*fathom* this."

And the whole class starts rolling. Like, there are claps. I freeze, face squinched and pencil on my notes, because what did I do? Why are these kids laughing at me? Am I in trouble?

I get my answer when Jack Pilgrim, the coolest, funniest kid in tenth grade, leans over three desks to pat me on the back. I get my other answer when the teacher screeches her chair across the floor, cutting through the laughter with, "Tutoring is after school until four thirty, Miss Etler. I'll see you then."

But I still don't get it. What was so funny? And what was so bad? Are we not supposed to say if we're confused?

Then, at driver's ed, it happens again. The driver's ed Poindexter is getting ten kinds of excited about Rule Number One: *Never* Take Your Eyes Off the Road. He's so into it, his hair is whipping around like an eggbeater. And I'm taking him seriously, especially since he showed us those slides of crushed cars with bloody arms and legs sticking out, all bent the wrong way. He's chanting it: "You *never* take your eyes off the road. Never, never ever take your eyes—" when it hits me that sometimes, you can't help it.

Before I even know I'm gonna say anything, I go, "What if you sneeze?"

His hair falls still. "What?" he asks, leaning left to see me around the big boy in front.

I lift my mug to hide from him and everybody. "If you

sneeze, your eyes close," I say. "You can't help it. You take your eyes off the road."

You'd think I'm the Beatles, the way the class cheers. I'm like, the conquering hero. And the poor teacher has to push the button for the next slide and wait for everyone to shut up, because you can't send kids to the principal on a Saturday morning. I feel so bad for him! But at the same time, I feel pretty great for me. 'Cause it's almost like they *like* me. Is this how Jack feels every day of his life? No wonder he says he doesn't need drugs to have fun.

But Jack *is* funny. Me? I'm not funny. I'm a weirdo who talks too much. And because I talk so much, some of the stuff that comes out happens to be funny. It's a law-of-averages thing.

The class I don't have to try in at all, though? Polly Skinner's English class. English is the anti-chemistry. Listen to it: Englishhh. It sounds like a baby blanket. Even the *G*, the one hard letter, comes out sounding wrapped in cotton. Not like chemistry, which is all bullet sounds and angles. *K! ISST! EE!* Chemistry is the alphabet version of a teacher rapping chalk on the board.

English, on the other hand, is whole life lip balm. For that one period a day, I feel like my clothes fit. Nothing's too tight, and nothing's so baggy it makes me look fatter. My brain, my body, my personality—everything—feels like it's okay.

Maybe it's because in English, I don't have to think about

myself. Mrs. Skinner makes learning so interesting, you disappear into it. Here's an example. She's teaching us to be good writers and says we have to show, not tell, what we're talking about.

She goes, "Think about Dial soap. It's hard and orange and rectangular. It's heavy in your hand. Can you feel it? Now, imagine someone takes away that Dial. They replace it with a bar of Dove soap. You can smell its perfume, can't you? Run your thumb over the Dove. It's soft as a cashmere sweater. Its edges are round and smooth as a woman's body. Now, feel yourself stepping into a shower and wetting the Dove. Feel the thick bubbles, the way the bar glides over your skin. Smell the perfume as it mists up into your hair. STOP! Replace the Dove with the Dial. Ouch! Your faces look like babies who got their binkies stolen!"

That feeling, she says, is what we need to bring to our writing. We need to make our readers feel as sexy—she said it!—as we did with Dove and as angry as we did with Dial.

Even when she has us do bookwork and vocabulary, with gourmet words like *lachrymose* and *hackneyed*, Mrs. Skinner's English class is paradise. My English homework doesn't even feel like work. It feels like eating candy. I get 100% on my vocab quizzes every time.

Mrs. Skinner gave us a writing assignment over the weekend. It was simple: describe a person you're seeing for the first time. That's it. When we have to pass our papers forward, I see other people's, and they all begin, like, "He is a tall man wearing a tie," then a couple more paragraphs like that. Mrs. Skinner is flipping through the stack, walking to her desk, when she goes, "Oh." She stops, and then she turns. "Class," she says. "Listen to this one." Then she reads it out loud.

Blue

Quick smile.
No words.
Black hair.
Two braids.
She doesn't wear makeup
But if she did
She'd still be beautiful.

It's about this girl I saw at my favorite CoDa meeting. I don't know her name. I don't even know why I called my paper "Blue." Or even what the blue means. So it's really kind of stupid. But Mrs. Skinner reads it out loud. And when she finishes, the class sits there, silent. Then Mia Esposito goes, "Wow." And then the other kids do too.

"Whose is it?" Whitney Lambourne asks.

Before I can stop her with my eyes, Mrs. Skinner goes, "Cyndy's."

They're all looking. At *me*. No Dunkin' mug's big enough to hide me from them all. Do they—do they *like* it?!

"Cyndy Etler?" says a guy's voice, and I internally combust.

"Indeed," says Mrs. Skinner.

And she puts down her stack of papers and picks up her teacher edition vocab book. And I sit there, wrapped in flames.

Okay, you won't believe what happened over Christmas vacation. I got a whole new life! And it's all thanks to Bitsy.

Bitsy is this lady at my Trumbull AA meetings. Everyone knows a Bitsy: She's got that haircut and body that mean she's super into tennis. She's tan all the time. And she never smiles, but always looks like she's smiling. That's Bitsy.

Anyway, one night I'm at my meeting, telling everyone how I know I'm an alcoholic even though I only drank that one time. How grateful I am to be sixteen years old with two and a half years of sobriety. Bitsy is listening really hard, I can tell. After the meeting she comes over and grabs my hand, then rocket launches into all these questions like, Did I really only drink one time? Did I do any drugs? Where was this place I got sober?

I'm honest with her, but it's a little scary, 'cause those creases in her face are getting deeper as I talk. I tell her what every Straightling knows: drugs don't make the druggie. But that's not the part she's interested in.

She's pulling a pad out of her purse and talking to herself, almost, like, "I would like to speak to your mother." Then she looks at me extra hard. "Did your mother make this decision? To place you in this—rehab?"

I nod and start to say how Straight saved my life, but Bitsy cuts me off.

"Okay, Cyndy." She anger-scribbles something on her pad, then rips off the page and hands it to me. "This is my number," she says, tapping one tan finger on her name. "You don't hesitate to call me. Night or day. I live nearby."

I wish there were words written on those lines on her face. I want to understand what she's really saying. We sit there kind of staring at each other for a sec; then she gets up and leaves.

Next time I see her, Bitsy seems pretty excited. She comes right up to me and says, "I want to tell you about another meeting I attend. It's called Overeaters Anonymous. OA. I find the meetings to be very supportive."

I sit there with my jaw dropped, because I *just* shared how I'm basically living on saltines, since the fridge is all moldy and it grosses me out.

Bitsy keeps talking. I'll never forget her words, because it's like she's a fairy godmother.

"My husband makes money. I can afford to do something nice for you. Would you be interested in seeing a nutritionist? A doctor who can tell you what you should be eating, to be healthy?"

I close my mouth and nod without exactly understanding what I'm agreeing to. I'm still stuck on "money...do something nice for you." I've never even imagined words like those.

"Would your mother take you?" she asks. "I'll pay for the appointment ahead of time, but I can't risk the liability of driving you myself."

"Ummm...I'll ask her?" I say.

"Great!" Bitsy says, like she's pumped to spend her money on me. And then she's gone, before I can even say thank you.

That was the beginning of my new life. I've basically switched to all OA meetings, but don't think I'm not still a druggie and alcoholic. I'm just a food addict too. I got on the eating plan from this really tough food rehab in Florida, so it's awesome. I know exactly what I'm allowed to eat and exactly what I can't ever touch again in my life. Here's how it goes:

Breakfast:

    1 cup puffed rice OR ½ cup plain

       cooked oatmeal

    1 cup skim milk

Lunch:

    4 ounces plain meat

2 cups plain cooked vegetables OR

   3 cups raw mixed salad

1 teaspoon margarine OR

   1 tablespoon fat-free dressing

Dinner:

4 ounces plain meat

2 cups plain cooked vegetables OR

   3 cups raw mixed salad

1 teaspoon margarine OR

   1 tablespoon fat-free dressing

Plus I get as much plain tea or coffee and as much Sweet'N Low as I want. And that's it. Easy, right? I have to be careful with salad dressings, because they can't have sugar in the first five ingredients. And I can't have any corn, peas, or potatoes. And of course no bread, crackers, cookies, cakes, ice cream, or candy. That stuff is a total drug for me.

The nutritionist gave me a way longer list of food I could eat, but I like the food rehab plan better, because it's so obvious. It's like riding on railroad tracks: all of the rules are set out for me in strong, hard lines. I can't steer wrong and lose my food sobriety when there're basically only three things I'm allowed to eat.

My druggie, foodie self still tries to win, though. Every day. Like, I'll shake my puffed rice out of the bag into the measuring cup, and every time, when I look at the cup from the side, I've humped the rice too high. I have to dump it out and repour it, making sure it scoops inward, so I'm getting a little *less* than a cup. That'll teach my druggie self to try to cheat.

The hard part is, my mother won't buy food for me anymore, which she announces the night before Christmas vacation ends. She's sitting at the table eating dinner when I go over to the grody fridge, which I have to use now, because my food plan has meat. I'm about to open it when she says, "I finished the hamburger." You can hear the clock ticking because she knows, and I know, that what I say next had better be careful.

"But…that was for my dinners."

"I'm aware of that, Cyndy. But you're so self-sufficient now, with your OA meetings and your weight loss, I've decided to let you be in charge of your own groceries as well."

There's this movie called *Mommie Dearest* I saw back before Straight. It's about an olden-days movie star who adopted a little girl and did really weird, cruel things to her. That movie pops back into my head as I stand there, paralyzed, with my hand on the open door of the fridge. I don't have any meat to eat, and there's only like a cup of lettuce left. But I'm starving! I gotta eat! Am I—am I going to lose my food sobriety? Maybe I could pick the noodles out of chicken noodle—

"Close that refrigerator door, young lady, unless you plan on paying the electric bill."

The sickest part was when the movie star went in the girl's closet and found her dresses on wire hangers instead of wood ones. She threw the dresses everywhere and beat that little girl with a hanger. My mother never hit me with a hanger, but still. I was hyperventilating as I fast-forwarded that scene.

Thank God, when my mother goes to bed, I find an old bag of green beans in the back of the freezer. I eat three cups of cooked vegetables instead of two that night, which is fucking scary. Talk about a slippery slope! But I tell myself that extra cup makes up for not eating any meat. And I get back at myself by not having any margarine.

Overall, though, our new system is working out okay. Here's the deal: my mother gives me twenty-five dollars a month for groceries, so I can't eat any of her food, but she can't eat mine, either. And she lets me ride with her when she goes to the grocery store. I just pray that we get there before someone else snatches up the meat with the orange mark-down sticker. It's gray instead of pink, and it smells funny, but it tastes okay after I fry it up with PAM. Otherwise, as long as I can find deep-discount generic frozen veggies and we go on double-coupon day, I can make the $6.50 a week cover everything.

If you think about it, she's actually, like, repeating the Straight phases, weaning me off of dependence on her for my food sobriety. So she's actually doing me a favor.

Except I might kill her over the Sweet'N Low. Do you know how much a box of that stuff costs? Almost half my monthly food allowance. And I use a lot of it, because it's my free food. So how is it fair for me to come downstairs and find six empty Sweet'N Low packets from *my* new box in front of the coffeemaker?

When my mother gets home from work, I ask her that question. Okay, I scream it. She answers by opening the front door, telling me what an ungrateful brat I am, and inviting me to find another mother who will tolerate my druggie bullshit. So now I steal handfuls of Sweet'N Low whenever I go to the diner with people after meetings.

The one thing that's scaring me, though, is maxi pads. Are maxi pads groceries? Because I totally just used my last one.

So I'm on a mission to not be the ultimate loser, right? And you wouldn't think my food sobriety would help my case. I mean, kids look at you funny when they offer you a Tic Tac and you *freak*, like, "Oh my God, no. I can't! Tic Tacs have *sugar* in them!" But actually, people seem to like me more since I started doing my food plan.

For example, Mr. Littberger. He must have been away at Dead shows or something, because I haven't seen him subbing at school for *months*. Then yesterday he's at the pay phones when I come in from the busses. When he sees me, he drops the phone and goes, "Whoa! Do you fool around?" Which makes me feel a little weird, because is that what the custom van is for? But still. Total compliment.

And in English class too. We're reading *A Streetcar Named*

Desire. Mrs. Skinner teaches drama the same way she teaches writing: when you walk in her room, you have to start pulling off clothes because it *is* 100-percent-humidity New Orleans. Mrs. Skinner *is* Blanche Dubois. You could drink her drawl like a milkshake.

I get to be Stella, and Mrs. Skinner's a frigging mind reader, because she gives Jack Pilgrim the part of Stanley. We're doing that scene where he's drunk and locked outside, and even though we're only reading, not acting it out, Jack Pilgrim is Jack Pilgrim. He pounds up from his desk yelling, "Stelllll-ahhhhh!" while ripping open his shirt. I. Swear. To. God. You can see his belly button. I'm frozen, staring, and Mrs. Skinner goes, "You cannot ignore a man's passion, Stella! Go to your husband!"

The stage directions say that I walk to him slowly, so that's what I do—like, for Mrs. Skinner, I mean. The stage directions also say that Stanley goes on his knees, puts his arms around Stella's middle, and puts his face on her hip. But even Jack Pilgrim isn't *that* Jack Pilgrim. At least, not with his girlfriend in the room. He puts his arms around my neck though, and his face on my shoulder. Which turns me into soft serve. No boy ever put his arms around my neck before I got on my food plan. Not one.

Not that I even come *close* to Jack's girlfriend, Whitney Lambourne. She's as tall as he is, and he's not short. And her hair makes her even taller. You know that hair band Poison? Her hair is totally the girl version. And she is skinn-nee.

Her middle is the same size as my wrist. I know I've gotten skinnier thanks to OA, *but…*

Whitney's a totally different type of pretty from Wendi Rosini, the other prettiest girl in our grade. Wendi has the kind of face you'd see on a museum wall in a fancy gold frame. Whitney's face is more like you see in the drugstore on a box of hair dye. I don't know which I'd rather be, but I get why Jack chose Whitney.

At the end of class, when I'm still melted ice cream from doing that scene with her boyfriend, Whitney comes up to me. The cheerleaders stop in the doorway to listen. But Whitney doesn't even care.

"Hey, what are you doing Saturday night?" she asks.

"I'mmm…nothing?" I say, clenching my mug handle so tight, it's gonna crack.

"Awesome, because my youth group is doing this not-Halloween costume party. You want to come?"

"Um, yeah, okay. Okay, yeah!"

The wind from the cheerleaders huffing out the door is almost enough to make Whitney's hair move. Almost.

So…Jack chose Whitney, not a cheerleader. So…some guys must like sweet more than sour.

At meetings, too, I'm suddenly popular. Meetings in the rich towns, even! My plan is working: now that I have my license, I can strategically force my mother to let me use her car to get to the cool meetings.

What really works is program-speak. And pulling out the M-word, which I save for special occasions. So I go, "Mom, doesn't Al-Anon tell you to let your addict meet their own needs? I need a CoDa meeting for my recovery. Shouldn't I drive myself, so you don't have to help me?"

Bingo. It's me, Madonna, and the Merritt Parkway, windows down and pedal to the metal. Holy fuck, am I glad I didn't suicide.

————

I've been *dreaming* of attending the Westport YP meeting, because I've heard rumors that actual young people go to it. Teenagers! In recovery! It's a super-miracle that I even get to go tonight because, of course, it meets on Saturday nights. But for once, my mother's boyfriends are all busy. And I'll have to send them thank-you notes, because there's not one but *two* sober boys at the Westport YP meeting. And both of them come over and talk to me! How am I suddenly living a Sweet Valley High book?

The first guy, John, is a Deadhead, legit. Anybody can wear a tie-dye and some string bracelets, but only a true Deadhead will put their scuzzy, long-toenail feet in Tevas and go out in public. When I tell John I can't really make it to this meeting because I live out in Monroe, he goes, "I could be your chariot." He says that to *me*. Cyndy Etler.

The other guy, Aaron, is more of a surfer. He has

lion-mane hair and a Ron Jon tank top. When I tell him I can't come back to this meeting he goes, "Yeah, I live up in Middletown. They won't be seeing me again, either." You can tell who's sweet and who's sour. But how come sour is shaped like He-Man and sweet is shaped like Grimace?

The three of us hang out, talking in the church parking lot until midnight. My mother is going to kill me. But Saturday night with two sober boys? No pressure to do things I don't want to, like with Jo's friends before Straight? Totally worth it. Hundred percent.

JULY 1988
ONE YEAR AND FOUR MONTHS OUT

Okay, I *really* need to get my own car. I've gotta be able to get down to the good meetings without my mother padlocking me. I need to be able to *do* things, like go to Connie's apartment, so she can help with my Smith College essay.

It's a given I'm going to Smith, I know that. It's destiny. I'll find which professor's office was my father's, and his ghost will meet me there, and we'll talk. He'll answer the questions I've been asking him in my head my whole life. He'll finally love me, or his ghost will, and that will fix everything. I'll be fixed. But even with destiny, you've gotta do some legwork. My legwork is writing this application essay. I need to make sure it's perfect, and Connie said she could help.

Connie's the one from CoDa I told you about, who drives the beat-up Jeep. She's also a fairy godmother, like

Bitsy. She hugged me after a meeting one time, and I told her she smelled frigging awesome. Next time I see her, she gets this big smile and pulls something wrapped in tissue out of her bag. A gift. For me. Instead of tearing it open, I try to be all ladylike, loosening the tape and folding back the tissue. And good thing, because what's inside is a heart-shaped glass bottle.

"'Crabtree and Evelyn Venetian Violet Flower Water,'" I read out loud. "Oh my God, it's delicious! Just the *words*: 'Flower Water.' I don't even care how it smells!"

"You *are* a writer," Connie says back, the most delicious words ever. "Now you'll smell like one too."

Connie did that for me *before* I went to OA and lost weight. She liked me even back then. But it turns out driving a Jeep isn't the coolest thing about her. Get this: she's a real, live writer. It's her *job* to write. Every day you can read her writing in the newspaper. My heart goes all speedy thinking about it.

Today will be the only time I'll complain about having my mother's car, promise. But today, I wish I didn't have my mother's car. Because if I didn't, I would've gotten to ride with Connie in her Jeep to her apartment. Instead, I follow her. But at least, since I'm not sitting next to her, I can scream when I see where she lives.

It's that huge Addams Family Victorian, right by the highway entrance in Norwalk. The one we drove by every day before we moved in with Jacque. I used to dream of living in that house, and now—what the fuck?—*Connie* does! She has the top floor as her apartment. The kitchen has slanted ceilings, and some of the windows are at the ends of their own little mini-hallways. It's all hers—she doesn't have kids or a husband or even a cat. It's just Connie, her apartment, and her writing.

I get to choose from twelve kinds of herbal tea, and Connie brings it to me in a red-and-white teacup on an actual saucer. There's a baby spoon in the red-and-white sugar bowl, and it *kills* me to not use it. The mangled Sweet'N Low I pull out of my pocket just isn't the same. I iron out the creases with a thumbnail as she reads my Smith essay.

"It's powerful," she says when she's done. "I can see why your father's dying before you could talk would be the event that most shaped your life. The admissions committee will see it too. Given your writing, a sewer rat would see it."

There's a *but* coming. I hear it, like a freight train. It's gonna flatten me.

"But you have to kill your babies."

"Connie! What?"

"Kill your babies. Scrap your writing. As writers, our words are our children. We birthed them; we adore them. But if they don't do their jobs, we have to kiss them goodbye."

"Okay, but you don't have to put it that way! That's a horrible way to describe it."

"But you won't forget it, will you? Now, they asked you for a moment; you gave them an event. How long is a moment?"

"Like, ten seconds?"

"And how long is an event?"

"A couple hours?"

"Exactly. Zoom in the camera. To stand out from the avalanche of admissions essays, you need to give them precisely what they've asked for: a moment."

"But how? I wasn't there the moment he died. Or even if I was, I don't remember. How am I gonna write about that moment?"

The Sweet'N Low packet chooses now to spring a leak. I've been squeezing all the powder into one pink corner and the paper there, fat with fake sugar and soft from my thumbs, gives up and splits open. Star-white powder explodes onto my lap.

"You're not. You're going to write about a moment you recall with the clarity of shattering ice."

"I am?" I say, rubbing the Sweet'N Low into my jeans.

"You are. Would you say that growing up without knowing your father has affected you?"

"Like, duh."

"Precisely. We're going to find a moment you would have experienced differently had you known your father. Then we'll use that moment to prove your point. Apologies for pressing on the bruise, but pain is real, and real sells. Agreed?"

59

"I talk about *every*thing at meetings. You know I'm okay with real."

"Bravo. Veracity is next to godliness."

Connie has me list all the ways not having my father has affected me:

- living in a crappy, embarrassing house
- getting embarrassing free lunch
- not getting designer jeans
- my mother marrying Jacque
- not having anyone to protect me
- not having anyone who loves me

But they all sound wicked whiny to me. Like I'm gonna tell Smith College that I didn't get Jordache jeans? Or that Jacque used to lock me in the bathroom with him? Not.

So Connie goes, "What about boys?"

"Boys?"

"Boys. Girls learn what to expect from boys from their fathers. You don't have a father, but you do interact with boys. This could be fertile ground. Good gracious, excuse the pun."

"The what?"

"Inside joke. Boys. Tell me about a moment you spent with a boy you like."

I can feel my grin cracking upward when she asks me that. Like, every single tooth is on display. I smile at my teacup for a sec, remembering. Then, because I know

Connie won't judge me, I close my eyes and go back there. I keep my eyes closed as I tell the story. Behind my eyelids, I get to live it again.

"It was in the rec hall at their church, Jack and Whitney's. It was a costume party, and I got there late. Everyone was over at the snack table. They had punch in a plastic bowl cut to look like crystal. Some kids' moms had made real cookies and cupcakes, you could tell by the Tupperware, but other moms bought the store kind. I walked in and saw all these kids' backs, because the snacks were on the other wall. But I couldn't recognize anyone. They all had on costumes."

"What was your costume?"

"I was an old maid. I mean, an old lady."

I want to look at Connie real quick to make sure she doesn't take that personal. But even more, I want to stay at the costume party. So I keep my eyes closed and switch my brain back to her question.

"I had on queen-size stockings, so they'd be baggy, and my mother's organ-player shoes. And this suit I'd found in a trunk in her room, from when she was in college. It was dark-green wool. The skirt went past my knees, and the jacket had brown leather buttons. It smelled like mothballs. It was perfect, except I couldn't button the jacket, because my mother has really small boobs. I had her reading glasses on and half a tub of baby powder in my hair, to make it gray. I stood there looking at these kids' backs, like, 'Fuck, I forgot to bring food,' when this prostitute turns around. Fishnets, huge high heels, tiny black roller derby shorts, and a red bustier. Like, totally *somebody's* druggie image. Just not mine. The prostitute walked over to me with her big, red lips all bunched up. I had no idea who she was, but when she got closer, I was like, 'Lady, shave your *arms*.'"

Connie laughs. "What does she do next?"

"She reaches out her hairy arm and honks my boob. And says, 'Nice falsies,' in Jack Pilgrim's voice."

Connie claps and my eyes fling open. Her face looks as happy as mine feels. "Truly? He squeezed your breast?"

"He didn't *squeeze* my *breast*, Connie! He *tweaked* my *boob*! And he didn't *think* he was—he thought they were fake!"

She raises her teacup in a salute. "To Jack, your cross-dressing beau!"

"It was his costume. It was like, Rocky Something Something Show."

"Cyndy, you have fine taste in friends."

"But I can't write about that for a college essay!"

"Perhaps not. But this is too good for a permanent killing. You must put it in a future piece. Promise me?"

"Promise you."

Two hours later, when I open the front door of my house, I get slammed by that feeling: I'm in trouble. All I can hear is the butcher block clock, ticking off the seconds. My mother said I had to be home by ten. It's ten.

There are so many dirty dishes, you can't tell if the sink is made of porcelain or metal. Bad sign. There's an overflowing Hefty bag leaning against the fridge, which means she heaved it out of the trash can by herself while I was out. Really bad sign. Her jacket and purse are on the table like she tried to go out, then remembered I had the car. Really, really bad sign.

I put the keys next to her purse all dainty, as if that's gonna turn back time. Then I tiptoe across the dining room. Maybe I can get in a pee before the bomb goes off.

Wasted effort.

My mother's in my bathroom. She's standing on the dirty little bathmat surrounded by every bottle of Silkience and Love's Baby Soft I ever saved up for. These bottles, and every other thing I keep under the sink, are lying sideways on the scungy, sticky floor.

"What *is* all this mess? This is ridiculous," she says.

"Ma. What are you doing with my stuff?"

"I need a pad. Just one pad, to get me through to when *I* can use *my* car to go to the store. Is that too much to ask?" Her jaw is clenched so hard I can see the outline of her skull. I'm in deep shit, because I'm out of super-maxis.

"I don't have any. I ran out. But I'll go to the store for you—"

"What do you mean, you 'ran out'? I spent fifteen dollars on that enormous pack of heavy-duties! What did you do with all of them?"

"That was last summer. Those are long gone."

"Last *summer*? Well, why didn't you tell me? Why didn't you get more?"

"I don't know, Ma. I just don't need them." Which is true. It's like, ever since I got food sober, God's been rewarding me by taking away my period.

"What do you *mean* you don't need them? Are you not— Cynthia Drew Etler! Are you *preg*—"

"No! God! I just—I don't need pads, okay? I don't want to talk about it!"

Her eyes sizzle into me like a branding iron, but then she remembers why she's here. She stalks off toward her car keys, walking like a cowboy. Then she turns.

"I have to tell you, I am *very* concerned. I will be calling Straight staff first thing in the morning to see what they have to say about this."

She grabs her keys and shoves out the front door with no daintiness whatsoever. Not even a little bit.

The doctor's office smells the same as it did when I was little: so clean it makes your nose squeak.

"Just slip into this smock. Opening in the front!" says the nurse, chipper as a tea-party hostess. How do you be so happy when your work's smell causes nosebleeds?

When I was little, my mother would lift me onto that giant paper towel that runs down the doctor's exam table. I didn't have to slide my own butt across it, ripping it in half.

I'm trying to fix the rip when the doctor **tap-taps** and opens the door. I'm leaning way over on my right butt cheek, pulling the ripped paper straight to clamp it in place with my left butt cheek, when he walks in. I slap back down onto cold, red leather.

"Hellooo, Cyndy. I'm Dr. Kretschmer. I understand you've stopped having your period."

He pushes his big pink hand at me. I look down as I shake it and watch my giant un-bra'd boobs slap each other under my tie-front doctor's-office dress. I don't talk, but he doesn't notice.

"Let's have you jump onto the scale for me," he says.

He sits on his rollie-wheel stool, spins away from me, and swooshes over to the scale, all in one motion. So I get down from the table, fist my dress-front closed, and step onto the scale. The doctor taps and clunks the metal bolts around. Finally, the lever stops moving.

"One twenty," he says.

Me? Cyndy Etler? One twenty?! I'm skinny! I must be skinny! I'm—

"What are you…five foot five?" he asks, his hand pushing me back against a ruler on the wall. "Five feet four inches. One hundred and twenty pounds. And you're—" He flips back some clipboard pages. "—sixteen years old. Two months away from seventeen. Congratulations!"

I haven't said a word, and he's ready to throw me a party.

"O-kay! Let's get ya back up here," he says, patting the paper towel.

I drill my eyes into the split in the paper, as if I could fuse the rip closed with my psychic powers. If there was no rip, I could get up there, like the doctor told me. But no *way* am

I shuffling my flabby butt and thighs across that table again, shredding the paper into confetti. I snatch a look at him, in case he's pulled out a little ladder to help me. But he's facing his cabinets, writing on his clipboard.

Quick, while he's not looking, I plant my hands on the edge, pretend it's the gymnastics vault, and *heave*. **RIIIP**. The sound of tearing paper makes the doctor turn around. Either that, or my face snapping into flames. There's zero way I can look at him, but luckily I don't have to. He's pointing down by my feet.

"Good girl. Let's get your feet in the stirrups here."

Stirrups. Like on a horse. But they're not by the ground, they're...sideways, in the air. Spread way apart.

I'm not wearing underwear.

The doctor stands at the foot of the bed, with his middle framed by the stirrups. He's patting the left one with his hand. It sounds like a tapping foot. **Tick-tock**. This feels ickily familiar.

I squinch my eyes shut and a number pops up: 120. 120! I weigh 120? Oh my God! Everything's perfect! I can do this!

I say my first word to him. "Okay."

I put one foot in a cold metal cup. It feels stuck. Trapped. But I'm 120. I'm light as a feather. I'm light as Wendi Rosini. My other leg is so light it flies up, then drops my foot into the other metal cup. My legs are spread open. I can't move them. And there's a man at the foot of the bed. I'm trapped.

But 120.

"Good girl," he says again.

Jacque has said those words to me in a gross fucking whisper. I can hear them in his sick accent. He'd be—*No!* I can't think about this shit! I have to just look at the ceiling. I have to be sane. I have to talk to myself. It's not Jacque's voice. I'm not in my bed. It's just Dr. Kretschmer.

I'm gushing sweat. Am I also going crazy?

"We're just going to check you out here," he says, holding up a metal shoehorn. "My apologies. This might be cold."

His rollie chair slides between my legs.

Then he's touching my z-z.

And pushing something inside me.

And splitting me in half.

I can't. I'm not. I can't…

"Okay!" he says. "You're fine." He pulls me empty, rolls backward, and disappears the shoehorn all at once. "All done! Go ahead and get dressed. I'll see you and your mother outside."

All done. He's gone. I'm soaked in sweat. As I climb off the table, I catch a whiff of myself, and *God.* I'm a Mrs. Skinner vocab word. I'm a cacophony of smells. Face smell, pit smell, and something-else smell. When I sit down to put my underwear back on, I feel like I might fall over. Like, what just happened?

But 120. I'm 120. I slide into my jeans so easy, it's like they're water. And everything's okay.

When I open the door to the hallway, Dr. Kretschmer's bringing my mother back from the waiting room. It's a small hall. The only thing here is another scale. So that's where we talk, next to the scale.

"Cyndy's fine," the doctor tells my mother. "But she's severely underweight at one hundred twenty pounds. That's what caused her period to stop."

"Oh!" my mother says. "But I weigh 118. Am *I* underweight too?"

"Well, it gets a little tricky. According to the body mass index, there's a range of acceptable weights for any given height. At Cyndy's five feet four inches, normal ranges from 110 to 150. Technically, she's within range. But individual norms differ. For her frame, her skeletal and muscular makeup, 120 is dramatically underweight. I'm not going to say she needs to gain weight; she looks fine, and according to the BMI, she's healthy. Instead, I'm going to put her on the birth control pill, which will force and regulate menstruation."

"Birth control?!" That's me *and* my mother.

"But pills are a drug! And I don't need—I'm a virgin!"

I can't believe I said that word. But it's true, right?

I don't remember doing sex, but there's a lot I don't remember from when I was little. I have certain memories that are freakishly strong, but they're an outline. Like, there's glass between me and the memory, and the panes are hazy. So even though I remember being alone in a dark room with

Jacque a lot, I don't remember what happened between the door closing behind him, and me being all alone again.

Why did I always *know* about sex, though? In third grade, I was the one who told the other kids how babies got made. God, I was *so* mean to Eve Yin, who was Korean. I was all, "Do you know where babies come from?" And Eve said, "Maybe...an egg?" Me and the other kids laughed at her so hard... I remember that, sharp as a steak knife, because it made the other kids like me. I remember Eve's voice going upward on *an egg?* But I don't remember who taught *me* the answer to that question.

I remember being in fifth grade and riding my Mongoose dirt bike on the back path, and coming down hard on a rock. The plastic seat bashed into my z–z, and I raced home to see if I had blood in my undies. I needed to know if my bike seat had made me lose my virginity. But there was no blood, and I had the same question then as I have today: Am I not a virgin? And like, why did I know blood and virginity went together? And why was virginity in my head when I was *ten*?

These are freaky thoughts. Normal people don't think like this. I have to try to be normal.

"It's okay," the doctor says, putting his hand on my shoulder. "The pill is frequently used to regulate the cycles of adolescent girls."

That doesn't make me feel any better.

When we get to the car, my mother starts frothing.

"One hundred and twenty pounds, Cyndy? I'm so proud of you! Your OA program is really working! Maybe I should give it a try…"

As soon as she starts talking, I close my eyes and lean back. I can't deal with her meaningful eye contact. It's a miracle, but she lets me get away with it. No pinched-leg, pulled-hair, "Look at me when I'm talking to you" today.

"And now the pill! My daughter is growing up!"

Behind my closed eyes, the blackout feeling rolls back. I squeeze tight against whatever window is trying to come unfogged. Keep it, memory. Keep it away from me.

That closet door in *The Lion, the Witch and the Wardrobe*, the one that led to Narnia? My version of that door is on Interstate 95. It's called exit 19. You go down the ramp and think you're in some regular town with trees, houses, a diner. Same old. But that's the thing about magic doorways—most people think they're nothing. It's only the bored and the desperate who look twice and find the magic.

When the diner's on the right, you turn left to go under the bridge, so I-95 is overhead. Ten seconds up the road, on the left, there's a white building with a huge wraparound parking lot. It looks like one of those clubs where war vets get drunk in the dark. And maybe it used to be, but not anymore. Now it's my Narnia: Club 12.

Bitsy was the one who told me about it, not like she's ever

been. Even though it's named after the twelve steps of AA, Club 12 isn't for boring, old alcoholics—you know, people who have been sober so long, it's just their lives. Bitsy heard about it from her daughter, who's young. Younger addicts, who still have some danger in them, we need excitement to stay sober. That's what Club 12 is for.

My first time I walk in late, of course, to the meeting that's being held there. It's so packed, people have to move so they don't get hit by the opening door. And every face—I swear, *every* face—turns away from the person sharing to check me out. Can I die now? Plus, there is *no* place to sit. My choices are either join the mob standing by the door or turn around and leave, with this whole convention of sober young people thinking, *What a loser.*

But Grant saves me. I don't know he's Grant yet, but it's obvious he's my savior. From over in the corner, I hear a *psst!* And there he is, with his half grin and his *c'mere* finger. I tiptoe through the crowd to reach him and, with his eyes on the guy who's sharing, he pats the linoleum counter next to him. For me. To put my butt there. My first Club 12 meeting, and my knees are practically touching this cute boy's shoulder. Like, okay. I can die now.

He doesn't look at me again until after the meeting. I'm flipping through the AA booklets on the counter next to me, as if I'm some dumb newcomer. I'll do anything to delay leaving this heaven and driving back to Monroe. From the corner of my eye, I see him pull out car keys. I try not to care.

But then. "Hi," I hear. I look up and it's all there: the half grin, the eyes, the shoulders. And it's all pointed at *me*. "Good meeting, huh?"

Oh my God, he's cute *and* he speaks my language.

"Oh, yeah. *Great* meeting. Lots of honesty, right?"

"Yeah, right. You new to the rooms? I haven't seen you before. I'm Grant, by the way." He holds out his hand to shake.

Can we stop and talk about this? First of all, he's my age. I don't care how square his shoulders are. You can't be eighteen and keep that baby face. So he's sixteen, and he greets people with a handshake? Nuh-uh. And second, what's he doing with that big gold ring on his hand? Third, thank you, Jesus God, for making me touch up my manicure last night.

"I'm Cyndy," I say, putting my hand in his. "Um, what else did you ask?"

I really said that. Wherever he learned he's supposed to shake hands, I'm not fit to sweep the floors. But he laughs. In a not-snotty way. He looks in my eyes, still holding my hand. Does this even happen outside of fiction?

"Nice to meet you, Cyndy." He squeezes and lets go. "I'm Grant. Wait, I said that." He looks at his keys and laughs again. He's got two key chains: a miniature flashlight and a chunk of wood. He curls his fist around the wood.

"Well, I better go. Work awaits. Nice to meet you, Cyndy. Keep coming back."

I watch his gray hoodie as he threads through the clots of postmeeting talkers. I cross my fingers and pray—I *pray*—he'll turn and say, "Can I have your number?" But he keeps going, out the same door I came in.

When I get home I go straight to my room because my mother's creepy old-man boyfriend is over. They're watching TV, and I'm *not* gonna be in the same room as them. He'd switch from watching TV to watching me. I put her car keys by her purse and yell, "Thanks, Ma," as I head upstairs.

What's extra-creepy is that my little sister's not home. Somehow in the divorce process, Jacque got visitation rights. So when I was at my meeting, my mother was here alone with old-man boyfriend. And *ewww*.

My mind needs something else to think about, *wicked* now. But I'm fucked because I finished my library book last night, and I'm not allowed any more food today, and I'm *not* going downstairs to shower, one wall away from where they're watching TV. If I had a friend to call, to talk to about Grant, I'd be millionaire happy. But nope.

My God, though. Can I really complain? This was my whole *life* in Straight: for a year and a half, 100 percent *nothing* except confessing what a scumbag I was and getting spit therapy. I couldn't walk down a hallway by myself. I couldn't read a cereal box! How the *fuck* did I... How did my brain not eat itself? I get that I needed to be beaten into accepting my addiction. But what about the fourteen months after that? Why'd I have to be in there so *long*?

Now that I'm out, I live like a Saudi prince. I drive a frigging car! I listen to music. I read actual books… I can open a door and step out*side*. Whenever I *want*. With no one even *watching* me. That's a frigging miracle.

So what the fuck am I saying, *I have nothing to do*? I have *every*thing to do. I have *any*thing. I have a window to climb out, a shingled ledge to sit on, and a zillion, trillion stars up over my head. I have cold air and trees and a love story to tell them about a lucky girl and the boy who shakes her hand. The boy named Grant.

12

I guess I believe in magic, but I didn't know magic could work this hard. If you saw the completely different person I am at Club 12, you'd *know* there's actual magic. The popular kids I need my Dunkin' mug to protect me from at school? That's who I *become* when I hit Club 12: pretty, happy, *popular!*

I get there late for my second meeting too. First thing I do while I'm smooshed by the door is scour the whole room with my eyes. When I get to the last face and still no Grant, my heart bombs down to my stomach. I end up sharing anyway though, because it's November 20. I share how three years ago today, my mother signed me into Straight, Inc., and how hard it was for me to accept that I'm an alcoholic and drug addict, since I only drank and drugged for two months before I got sober. And I share how now, by the grace of God and these rooms, I have three years' sobriety *and* I have food sobriety. I swear, the roof is rattling when they all clap for me. I get like ninety-six hugs at the end of the meeting.

And then, when I'm walking out the door to the parking lot, guess who's walking in? Our eyes meet, and his eyebrows jump, and his smile goes up on *both* sides. Because of *me*. He hooks his arm through mine, like he's Frank Si-fucking-natra, and I look down because what do I do with my *face*? And *ting!* His gold ring is glowing in the floodlight. A conversation piece from God.

"Hey, lady!" he says, which is way cuter than, "Why do you wear this ring?" which is what I say. He laughs and leaves his arm where it is, like I'm not an epic buzzkill.

"Oh God, this *ring*," he says. "*Why* do I wear it, or what *is* it? What do you really want to know? I have a strict one-question policy."

As he talks he slides his arm down, grabs my hand, and starts swinging our arms like we're skipping little kids. I totally get it, Juliet. I'd dagger myself to stay with this guy too.

"But first, my question," he says. "Which one's yours?" He waves our arms at the parking lot.

"Um, that one. The one that looks like a cop car," I say. "It's my mother's."

"Sweet. A cop car. We'll be totally safe."

He leans back on the hood like it's *his* car. I lean next to him like this is something that happens to me.

"Did you decide which question?" He tilts his head to look me in the eyes. The way guys do in movies before they kiss the girl.

My real question is, *When's the last time I brushed my teeth?* The question I ask is, "*What* is that ring?"

"That's what I thought you meant," he says, and lets go of my hand. Which makes me want to cry for a sec, until he pulls off his ring, spreads my fingers open, and puts it in my palm. It's the exact weight of a human heart. He shines his key chain flashlight on it, so I can see the shield pressed into the flat, oval top. "It's the Lattimore family crest," he says. "Cough, cough, right?"

"Your family has a *crest*? You're royalty?"

"No, no. It's stupid, really. Just, one of my ancestors was a war hero."

We both stay quiet and think about that. His voice says no big, but his face—what I can see of it above the flashlight—says something different. It says he could just hand me his family ring, instead of clutching it so tight it punctured his fist. It says he could grab my hand with zero fear I'd pull away. It says he's worth something and he knows it, so he can pretend he's nothing special. I think to tell him my father was a famous composer, but the words feel like a puff of smoke. He's got proof of what he is. I've got dreams of what I could have been. We're *so* not in the same league.

"Oh good, you're still here!"

He scoops his ring out of my hand as we both look up, like kids caught in the cookie stash.

A lady in Guess jeans and a hippieish purple Indian top is standing in front of us, saying, "I really wanted to catch you, Cyndy. I loved hearing you share. I'm Suzanne." She puts her hand out, then goes, "Can I hug you? Let me hug you. You're a little miniature me! Oh, if I'd had your wisdom when I was your age!"

"Hi, Suzanne," I say, hugging her back. She doesn't smell like violet flower water, but she looks like she should.

She gives a quick hi to Grant, then looks back at me. "Three years sober today! And you're how old?"

"I just turned seventeen."

"So you've been sober since you were fourteen! You're the Buddha of AA! Do you—can I ask if you have a sponsor?"

"Um, not really. I haven't found the right—"

"I get it. Picking a sponsor is a big deal. I don't have a sponsee right now, so let me give you my number. If you want to keep that sobriety, you've got to have a sponsor!"

"Right. Thanks," I say, taking the card from her. She wrote the *S* and the *Z* so swoopy, you'd think she was a movie star. I'm grateful she's making me look popular, but I'm ripshit she's hijacking my Grant time.

"Okay, Cyndy. *Great* to meet you. Give me a call!" she says, and gets into a pearl-colored convertible.

"Get a sponsor! Work the steps! Take it one day at a

time!" Grants squeaks in a lady-voice, clicking and unclicking his little flashlight. His family ring is back on his finger.

He's like, mocking the program. I didn't even know that was possible. "You don't believe in that stuff?"

"Nah, not really. I mean, I come to meetings at Club 12 when I have time. But otherwise, I stay sober because I want to stay sober, not because some dead old man in a crusty book tells me to 'search out the flaws in my makeup.' Life's too short, you know?"

"Yeah, I guess," I say.

If he comes to meetings when he has time, what if he runs out of time?

"Speaking of meetings, I guess I should go into that one," he says, thumbing at the Club 12 building.

If he goes in there, I might never see him again.

"Yeah, I guess," I say.

"You did the early meeting, right?" he asks.

If I lie and say no, he'll ask why I was walking out before.

"Yeah," I say.

"Okay, well...see you next time," he says, and gives me a two-finger salute.

I want to chase after him, to sit on the counter with my knees at his shoulders. I want to link his arm through my arm, to put my hand in his hand. I want to go back to our movie-kiss moment. I *want*. But I have to hide it. That want is the ugliest thing in the world.

I'm allowed to want a sponsor though. I pull Suzanne's card out of my pocket, put it up to my nose, and inhale deep. It smells like a second-place ribbon.

Even though they're her boyfriends, sometimes my mother's latest buys stuff for me. Which I don't get. If I had money to burn, I'd spend it on Benetton sweaters and Coach bags for my*self*. Buying a baked potato and grilled cheese for some lady's kids is, like, equal to or less than spending ten bucks on toilet paper. Shoot. At least the toilet paper does something for you.

It's more than ten bucks, actually, because I don't just get the baked potato (which is legal now! Since I reached goal weight, my food plan lets me have one starchy vegetable twice a week!). I also have the steamed broccoli and the half a roasted chicken, which is one of the most expensive things on the whole Monroe Diner menu.

The heaven of food cooked by someone else cancels out

my feeling bad for old-man boyfriend spending money on me. It even cancels out my conscience, which is barking, "You *know* if you put that chicken on a food scale it's gonna weigh more than four ounces." I bark back, "I don't *have* a food scale at the Monroe Diner, and I think I know what four ounces looks like by now!" Then I quick-eat that pile of chicken before my conscience can stop me. I'm like Henry VIII, tearing the little bones apart to get every last sliver.

I'm finishing cleaning my bones when my mother goes, "*You* are a *mess!*" I look up, but she's talking to the other mess, my little sister. "Come on," my mother says, picking her up from her booster seat. "We're going to the bathroom."

I want to say, "Don't leave me alone with him!" But I can't because she's got her mad voice on. So I turn my head and finish licking the grease off my fingers.

She's three steps away when old-man boyfriend leans into me and says, "I bet you've got the tastiest fingers in town!"

I jam those fingers *right* under my new Guess jeans, grease and all. I don't even care. I turn my head even farther away, so hard it hurts, and close my eyes and hold my breath. And I stay there, paralyzed, until my mother gets back from the bathroom.

"Come on. We're leaving," she goes, still mad about my messy little sister. I hang back from them as long as I can, stacking the dishes for the waitress. I have to mentally bulldoze myself into his car for the ride home.

But anyway, Guess jeans! Grease stripes or not, they're *real* Guess, ankle zips and all. Size eight! They were a gift from my mother's other boyfriend, the Japanese man. He doesn't say very much, and every time he comes over, he's wearing a suit and tie. Don't ask me where my mother finds these guys, but she told this one that I got down to a size eight and that she's all proud. Then, next time he comes over, he holds out this Macy's bag. With *Guess jeans* inside. That boyfriend, I actually hugged by choice.

I wear my Guess every single day now, along with a man's button-down from the thrift store. I pretty much have just this one outfit, like a frigging Smurf. But at least that outfit's cool. I copied it from my sponsor. Yes, really! That lady Suzanne who asked if I needed a sponsor? She's mine now!

Mine. Isn't that a nice word? It makes me feel all cozy, like me and my mine are together in a little box, the kind they put your earrings in if you buy them at the jewelry store. We're tucked in there together on that square cotton pad, and God or somebody is fitting the box lid back on, so it makes that soft cardboard *click* as it closes. And everything feels safe, and everything's okay.

Having a sponsor is like having a mini, one-person Straight group. As a fellow addict, she totally gets my issues. She gets that everything—home, school, Straight, sobriety—is terrifying, and all that terror makes me want to put something in my mouth. Her job is to make sure my mouth stays empty.

Even though she's an alcoholic, I talk to my sponsor about food stuff too. The twelve steps are the twelve steps. They work with every addiction. But I don't know if I'm supposed to talk to her about the other stuff, like my mother and her boyfriends and the cheerleaders and all. I mean, Suzanne always has on a *choice* outfit. Her lipstick never wears off. She's the kind of skinny where she doesn't have to try. I don't think she can necessarily relate to my problems, you know? And I need her to keep liking me. So I'm going to keep my life-life hidden from her.

What I extra won't talk to her about is Grant, because I can't even hear what she'd say about him: "You're not ready for a relationship." Program people *love* to use that line, to pretend they're further ahead than you. It should be on the wall in calligraphy, next to *First Things First* and *Just For Today*.

You're Not Ready For a Relationship

I don't care what they say. I love my program people, but I don't love them enough to give up the best part of Narnia: Turkish Delight.

Ever since I first read *The Lion, The Witch and The Wardrobe*, my mouth has had this memory of Turkish Delight. I can see the word spelled out in my head: *NOUGAT*. I can feel the pillowy rectangles, studded with pistachios, packed like bricks in a waxy paper box. Turkish Delight is better than money or hugs or program people. I'd do anything to get some.

And…Grant kissed me. And it was Turkish Delight.

I go to another Club 12 meeting, right? But this time, I'm wearing Guess jeans. So I look pretty good. I walk in and he's sitting on his same barstool, so I spend the meeting on the counter next to him, with my legs almost touching his shoulders. Halfway through the meeting, he—oh, my God—he starts pulling the zipper on my ankle up and down. Still looking at the speaker but totally touching my leg.

After the meeting, we lean on my mother's cop car so long, talking, everyone else takes off. I'm holding his block-of-wood key chain, running my fingers over the letters carved into it. He says they spell out GRANT, but the *T* and part of the *N* fell off.

I'm telling him, "It doesn't actually say 'GRANT,' it says 'GRAN,'" when he puts his fingers under my chin and tilts my head up. He looks at me—he looks at my chin, my cheeks, my eyes, and he kind of sighs as he leans forward and kisses me. On the lips. His sigh comes out the sides of his mouth, because he doesn't keep his lips still. He turns his head sideways so our lips make an *X*, and he makes his mouth bigger and smaller, and then he…he sort of traces my lips with his tongue, which—oh my God—makes me almost fall down to a praying position. And then, while still holding my chin, he pulls his beautiful family-crest face back and looks at my lips. His hand is magically holding up all 120 pounds of me, and he goes, "I'm sorry."

My mouth is hanging open with drool all spilling out, so my "What?!" sounds more like my tonsils clicking around in my throat. Which must gross him out, because he lets go of my chin. He leans back on the car and folds his arms across his chest. His ring flashes at me like a stop sign.

"I shouldn't have done that," he tells the pavement. "I'm sorry."

I've tucked the drool back in, so I can speak, sort of. "Wha—you don't have to—"

"No, really," he says, looking back up at me. "I shouldn't have done that. I have a girlfriend."

Where did he have those boxing gloves hidden? He hit me with 'em, right in the face. The exact face he was just *gazing* at, like it was some rare artifact. I turn away and start batting my eyelashes, as if that's gonna scare the tears from showing up. But Grant doesn't even care. I can hear it from his sniff. He's—he's crying?

I whip around to check, and yeah. He's not, like, bawling, but he's pulling a hanky—a cloth frigging hanky—out of his corduroys' pocket, and pinching the bridge of his nose with it. He's guy crying.

"Oh my God, Grant! It's okay!" I say from where I'm suddenly standing, toe-to-toe with him.

He ducks his face and jams the hanky back in his pocket, because he's mortified. He's friggin' crying, and I'm all in his face. How did I get so stupid? I start to turn away, to give him his privacy, but he grabs me in a hug. And ooohhhhhhh my God.

    Nothing.

       has.

          ever.

            felt.

               this.

                  goooood.

"I'm so sorry," he mumbles into my hair.

"It's okay," I whisper back, praying he doesn't feel spittle. I mean, God. He's a cute sober boy with a gold family ring. So it's okay. Doesn't he know this? Anything he does. It's okay.

He squeezes me harder. So I say it again. "It's okay, it's okay. It's okay."

I don't get any more Turkish Delight before he leaves, but I do get something else unbelievable: a card. A business card.

"This is where I work," he says, clicking his little flashlight and shining it down on the card.

It has a picture of a shelf with some cans, a counter with a cash register, and the words "Sinclair's Grocery." Underneath it says, "Grant Lattimore." Under that there's a phone number. A *phone number*!

I touch my finger to the bumpy, glossy edges of the cash register. The store where he works is so rich, their business cards are 3-D. And he's inviting me into his world. His perfect-name, perfect-family, perfect-job world.

When you're perfect, of course you have a girlfriend. And she's perfect too. Like, blond braid down a suntanned back, bikini with a sleeveless Izod over it, no makeup except pink Bonnie Bell. Because that's the kind of girl who gets a Grant. We all know it. And Grant can't help it. It's that science-nature law. Darwin.

In case you haven't taken bio yet, here's Darwin's law: the best, strongest boy squirrel gets the best, prettiest girl squirrel, and they have the superbest babies, who get the meatiest nuts. And it keeps going that way. Because the best can choose the best, and their offspring are the ones that survive, because they have the best genes. The lame, weak, and ugly squirrels die off eventually because the strong squirrels don't choose them. Their babies don't get the strong genes that can beat nature and keep their family line going.

Same with humans. The best stay with the best, because if you could choose anyone, why would you choose the less best? Grant's girlfriend probably has lace underwear with her family crest on them. Their kids will have family crest private planes.

I don't come from a family like that. At least not now, I don't. It seems like I started out there, with the big-deal dad and the Smith-graduate mother, but my Darwin ranking got shuffled along the way. Maybe my father wasn't a strong enough squirrel, which is why he died early. Or maybe my mother looks superior on the outside, but she's inferior on the inside. Whatever got fucked, I'm nowhere near Grant's squirrel level now. I'm just lucky he'll hang out on the low branch with me. But if he'll feed me Turkish Delight while he's down here, my low branch will feel as high as frigging heaven.

14

MARCH 1989
TWO YEARS OUT

My sponsor, Suzanne, is the grownup version of Grant's girlfriend. I know because I'm at her family's house. It's this holy-shit-it's-actually-warm-out day, so they've got the living room glass doors open to the backyard. But they're not the plain glass doors that slide sideways, like at my house. They're the kind with the tic-tac-toe pattern in them, the kind that open outward, like at the frigging White House. My sponsor, her mother, and her sister are all in bare feet with white cotton dresses, all light and smooth and tiny. You can tell how everything in their life works: like dolphins cutting arcs through water.

Suzanne invited me over to work on a "fearless and searching moral inventory." Um, gag me? She calls a moral inventory the fourth step. I call it an M.I., just like every other Straightling does. That's one part of Straight I don't miss: the 486 M.I.s I had to write, one for every day I was in there. And now I have to do a 487th?

But when you're me, you don't turn down an invitation to get the fuck out of the house. Especially when the invitation comes from another program person, who doesn't think you're an alien freak from planet recovery. I'll do the 487th M.I. Whatever it takes.

But here's what I don't get. Jack Pilgrim, who's as big a freak as I am, is this, like, social success story. Shit, he's maybe *more* of a freak than me. Last week, he and his new best friend, this kid Roger who just moved here, came to school in *hazmat suits*. Swear to God. Face masks, breathing stubs, and florescent biohazard signs on their backs. Did they explain why? No. Is this total freak behavior? Yes. Did everybody *love* it? Abso-frigging-lutely. So how come my freakiness makes me the school reject?

Really, though, I hardly go to school anymore. My mother's so caught up in her love life, she doesn't even notice if I stay in bed. She only makes me go two or three days a week. It sucks to get math tests back with twenties on them, and Mrs. Skinner is, like, sad at me. But I can't keep walking past the hallway's popular zone, where laughy Brent and mean Kathy hang out. I can't keep getting lasered by their eyes and their words, which I can never quite hear. If I had just one person who got me—even if we didn't have class together, if we could just sit together at lunch—I could get through the school day. But being the lone ranger inside these boiling, crowded school walls is death. No, it's worse. It's being *alive* for your death.

And on top of all this, my mother's in this phase where she's mad about me taking her car, so I can't get to the cool meetings. And I've been getting sick of Trumbull AA, so I don't feel like getting rides there from the old AAers. But then Whitney asks if I want to go with her and Jack to their church's youth group meeting one Sunday night. So I'm like, what the fuck. Okay, if I can get a ride.

The youth group meeting itself isn't so bad. We sit in a circle and talk about some Bible verses and how they relate to our lives. In a way, it's like being in group at Straight, except nobody here is screaming or spitting in anyone's face or talking about why they hate themselves. And nobody bum-rushes a misbehavior and slams her to the ground, so her skull makes that **CRACK** on the tiles. Okay, maybe youth group isn't that much like Straight group. But we do sing a few songs.

Maybe I would've gone again if I didn't socially slaughter myself afterward. Jack and Whitney go into the rec hall for the post-group juice and cookies, which of course, I can't touch. I don't even want to deal with the whole "no, I'll stand here by myself with this small cup of water" scene, so I scurry off to my handy-dandy hidey-hole, the girls' lav. But this lav is in a church, with no teachers around to spy and snitch. So it's more of a dragon's lair than a bathroom.

I push open the door and get punched back by this planet-sized gust of smoke. Thank God it's just cigarette smoke, but still. If you're smoking in the girls' room, you're breaking the rules, and breaking the rules is the first step toward a slip. I can't jeopardize my sobriety like that! Except I've already opened the door, so I can't not go in. My face is an *ABC After-School Special*, all pinched like, *Oooh, shit!* I know it is, because I'm petrified. This is exactly what Straight warns you about: being in closed spaces with bad influencers.

You know what's even scarier than losing my sobriety? Being Loser Etler *again*. Other kids can somehow not spaz in dangerous peer situations, so I need to not fucking spaz as well. I walk through the smoke blast, and there's Mary and Donna, sitting on the heater by the window, which is cracked open.

"Hey, Cyndy!" says Mary, holding her cigarette out all awkward and wrong. "Want a puff?"

A *puff*. We *are* in an *ABC After-School Special*.

"Yeah, it's cool! Come on!" goes Donna, leaning away from the cig like it's got bad breath.

"Yeah, no. I just have to…" I say, and slam the handicap stall door shut behind me. They know the rule, right? You don't talk to the peeing person. You pretend you forgot she's there.

They're stone silent as I unzip my jeans and uncrinkle

a paper seat cover. It's like they forgot I'm here, but they forgot each other is here too. So we're all listening to my quiet, pushing effort to eke out a pee.

No dice. The silence is so total, I can hear the paper sizzle-burning down the un-dragged cigarette. I can picture the long, dry tube of ash sagging off its end. Mary doesn't know to tap it. If she did, I'd have heard the little **bap-bap-bap**. It's *that* silent in here.

I can't produce a pee, and that tube of ash—I *know* it's there—is killing me. I have a sudden, crushing need to bust out of my stall and snatch the smoke out of Mary's hand. And tap it. Three times. While staring her in the eye. Like, *this* is how it's done. Then I'd either smoke or eat the rest of the cigarette before hauling ass out of that church.

Instead I creak-roll off some toilet paper, wipe my bone-dry folds, and flush. Finally, there's some noise in the room.

When I come out of the stall, the ash is two miles long. Just like I said.

"You sure you don't want, Cyndy?" goes Donna.

I look at the floor, instead of at that ash. The fuck do I explain sobriety, Straight, Inc., and the slippery slope of druggie ties that would yank me back to using? Or how *good* it would feel to sit on that heater, holding that smoke the *right* way, instead of standing around dumbfounded, like a fucking weirdo? How do I explain how that cigarette would save me and kill me all at the same time?

"I—I can't," I say instead. "Because of God."

And I run out of that bathroom so hard I hit myself in the face with the door. The sharp shock of it keeps me from hearing Mary's and Donna's laughter. From knowing they're gonna tell the whole school, "God told Cyndy Etler to stay away from cigarettes."

I've got to get it through my head: just because someone's a church person, doesn't mean they're a God person. For me, my program is all about my friendship with God. We're so close, I could tell you what color tie He's wearing today. And program people talk about their relationship with God too, all the time. So I walk around with this assumption that everybody who wears a cross has the same sort of…I don't know, God-ness. That they're truly nice. That they follow the rules. That they try to make other people feel good. So I keep thinking I can be friends with kids who are in church youth group. And I keep finding out that I'm wrong.

Really, the kids who wear their crosses outside their collars so you notice them are the *meanest*. They're the ones who make sure you know when they're laughing at you. Jack and Whitney are truly nice, and they really don't drink or do drugs, but all these other youth group kids? All they talk about is partying.

Like, why did Mary and Donna try so hard to get me to smoke? What are they, on Satan's payroll? I won't give in to temptation, though. One cigarette and I'd be *right* back in my druggie past, because that's how strong my addiction is. *Nothing* could make me desperate enough to smoke.

Except the fact that, outside of that one hellacious youth group meeting, I was at Club 12 like every night before my mom got weird about the car. And Grant never showed. Not once. It's like he doesn't want to see me. Which I can't handle. That could be enough to make me smoke. Maybe I should go to his grocery store and buy a pack of Marlboros.

Oh my God, see what I'm saying? See how bad I need God in my life? Left to my own devices, I am *fucked*. So thank God I get to be here at my sponsor's tidy, delicate, rich-people's house today, even though I feel like a whale trying to walk on its hind legs. At least here, my whale song is answered by her family's dolphin song. They're all in recovery, Suzanne and her sister and her mother. So even though I'm not sleek and smooth and dressed in white, at least I kind of sound like them when we talk about the program. Dolphins and whales, we're both underwater singers. We understand each other. The youth group kids, though—I have to give up that hope. They can't be my friends. They don't speak sober.

15

I fucked up. I really did. It's like I was possessed or something. I could see what I was doing, but I couldn't stop myself.

It's a random Thursday, right? I'm coming down the stairs as my mother's hanging up the phone. And she's *giggling*, which—*grody*. And she goes, "Why don't you take the car out for a while. You just have to put gas in it."

And then, lickety-split, I'm on 95. I'm driving to exit 19, even though it's 3:00 p.m. and there's totally no meeting this afternoon. I turn right off the exit instead of left, and I drive down these perfect streets with perfect homes and perfect little stores, where they sell herbal tea and white cotton dresses and wooden key chains carved with family crest names.

And it's *right here*, this soft, easy life. It's right in front of me. It's have-able, because all of these elegant Southport,

Westport, Fairfield people *have* it. And I could've had it too, if my father had kept being famous and composing music, instead of dropping dead. And if I had that life, everything would be perfect. So I'm trying really hard to be thin enough to fit through that fissure, that crack at exit 19 that separates hard-dark-mean from soft-safe-easy.

But I can't seem to make it work. There's an invisible wall. I can drive down these streets. I can see the perfect people. I can even visit their houses or go into their stores, like Pier 1 or the Gap. But it's a force-fit. I'm the clunky Toughskins preschooler who tries too hard, who jams the toy truck through the dollhouse's front door. The one who wrecks the door *plus* the whole front wall of the dollhouse and pisses off all the other preschoolers. Stupid kid! Don't you know trucks are for the *dump*, not for houses?

But like I said. I can see what I'm doing, I just can't stop myself.

So I'm driving down these streets, looking at the ever-green windowsills, the black door frames, the heavy cloth curtains hung from metal O's that clack against the curtain rods when they get pulled shut at closing. Their stores are set up to feel like houses. They're another place for Westport people to feel safe. I drive stupid slow, studying the decorated shop windows, the doors with their brass flaps for the mail to slide through. You can tell when a store sells the kind of stuff women like, because they have a puffy armchair visible from the street with a reading lamp next to it. A few stores even have chimneys with actual smoke coming out the top.

This is why Grant is so confident. Because he's from here, this place where *every* place is a home. There's always a fire in the fireplace and fresh milk in the fridge. And Grant and his fellow Westporters are always welcomed inside with a smile and, like, some bedroom slippers. How could he not feel sure the world loves him?

The sun is starting to go down. The sky is getting darker. I should drive to the beach and watch the sunset. It would be heaven, because it's too cold for anyone to be there, staring at me and my cop car. I could walk in the sand and pretend I'm smoking a cigarette. But that stupid, clumsy preschool kid, she never does what she should. Instead, she has to force herself into the games where the other kids don't want her.

I drive under a cobblestone railroad bridge and come out on the chicest street yet. And there it is: Sinclair's Grocery. The letters are stenciled across the window. Through it, I can see wooden shelves lined with cans and boxes. My heart goes flash-frozen: it's one of Grant's homes. And I'm gonna shove a dump truck through the front door.

I park down the street from the store so my heart can thaw before Grant sees me. Is it even safe to leave a crap car among the Volvos and Rovers, or does it automatically get towed? Safety doesn't matter, though. Like I said: I have no choice. This is fate at work.

Skinny ladies with cashmere shawls and pearl earrings click past me, arrowing their gazes straight ahead. If I were in L.L. Bean cords and an Irish wool sweater, I might get a glance, even with my big, big hair. But Guess jeans and a sweatshirt? Clearly, I should be somewhere else. The ladies tell me so by pretending they don't see me.

My brain is a scribble as I step onto Sinclair's front step, a slab of rock that dates back to the pilgrims. There's an inch of air between the door's base and the floor; I can feel the heat on my toes. Sinclair's can afford to heat the sidewalk because Sinclair's charges three bucks for a piece of penny candy.

The thumb-latch door handle is soft and warm. It clacks so loud, the cashmere street ladies turn and look. And so does Grant, from his spot behind the wooden counter, next to the antique circle-button cash register. The same cash register as on the business card he gave me.

When Grant sees me, he drops his smile and gets down from the stool he's sitting on. For once, he looks nervous. God, can I relate.

"Um, hey," I say, but I doubt he hears me over the bell clanging on its ribbon above the door. I'm half-in and half-out of the store, my front boiling with shame and my back frozen with fear.

"Yeah," he says, glancing around the empty store. "Hey." Grant Lattimore is speechless. First time ever.

"I was, you know… I thought I'd just…" I try again.

"Yeah. Yeah."

"Um, want me to… I'll close the door."

The bell kicks up again as I push the door closed. Somewhere behind Grant, a phone starts ringing. He closes his eyes, and you *know* he's thanking God.

"I gotta get that." He ducks back through a doorway. Then I hear, "Sinclair's, Grant speaking," like he's been saying it since birth. Like he has no fear of doing it wrong. "Yup. Ordered it just for you. I'll pull a few boxes and hold 'em behind the counter… Anytime."

I hear the solid **click** of Grant hanging up, but I don't hear him move. That customer on the phone—he talked to her like a grandma. Mr. Sinclair trusts Grant with the whole store and register, like a rich uncle. Grant of a thousand homes. Grant of a thousand families. Grant of the lips made of Turkish Delight.

Grant who wishes I would leave.

The store's so quiet, we can hear the creaking floorboards under my feet. The creak wakes Grant from his daze. He comes back through the doorway with a new kind of smile: a businessman's smile—no teeth, narrow eyes.

"So. What can I do for you?" he asks, leaning one hand in a tent shape on his stool.

"I—um, I thought there was, but there's no meeting at Club 12, so I—I came to buy some cigarettes."

"Okeydoke. I didn't take you for a smoker, but that's your biz. What's your poison?"

"No, I'm not really. I just—my what?"

"Your brand. What brand of cigarettes." He's got his back to me, with his arm raised to grab my smokes and fling them out the door so I'll chase them like a dog.

"Oh, ah—Marlboro, it was. Marlboro reds." They're probably like ten bucks here. Holy fuck, I better have enough money. Do I have enough? Holy fuck, holy f—

"Here ya go. On the house," he says, snapping a pack on the counter. "Matches?" He thumbs at a flat box by the register. I tweeze out a pack of matches with two fingers; the cover has the same antique cash register picture as his card. *Sinclair's Grocery*, the matchbook says. I'll never burn one of these matches. Not ever.

"Okay, well," he says.

And he's saved by the bell again, as a Lauren Bacall lookalike swings open the door. **CLING-A-CLING-A-CLING!** goes the bell.

She's got one of those furs around her neck, the kind with the animal's face still attached. "Grant, darling!"

When she says that, Grant's real smile comes back.

"And who's your little...?" Ms. Bacall asks, smiling through her frost-brown lipstick. She's somehow looking down at me even though we're the same height.

"Oh, no. She's not... See you 'round," he says to me, and I'm dismissed. The bell doesn't even tinkle for me when I leave.

The cold outside is a whole-body douche. *That's* where

I want to be? *That's* who I want to belong with? Frosty pinched lips and business-squint eyes?

I slap the Marlboros on my palm bone, and *God*, does it feel good. It's hard. It hurts. It feels *great*.

It's really dark now. The cashmere ladies have been joined by their wingtip men. The box-on-bone sound is freaking them out, you can tell, because they're *looking* at me now, with lips in the shape of *Oh my*. Fuck them. Fuck trying to squeeze through the crack into their lives. Fuck their cobblestones and their old-timey grocery stores and their hush-bitter voices.

Ripping the thin cellophane off the lid of my on-the-house Marlboros, I lean back on the cop car's hood. The cigs are packed tight under the lid. They smell like untapped love. Like hope and freedom and Bridgeport, my scungy anti-Westport, the city where I stayed before Straight. The lid snaps down over the rows of cigarettes; the Sinclair's matchbook tucks behind the cellophane wrapper.

When we were doing *Streetcar*, Mrs. Skinner taught us the vocab that goes with proper Southern mores. Gorgeous words: *aghast, repugnant, befoul*. Words for disgust. Words that are perfect for Westport. I could disoblige Westport by lighting a Marlboro. I could befoul the air with my gauche. But I won't. That Turkish Delight kid, he didn't get to stay in Narnia, and I don't either.

Okay, *this* you're not going to believe. Club 12—*my* Club 12—on Saturday nights? *Dances.* Sober dances. Every Saturday! All sober people! I don't even know how I went this long without knowing. It's as if everyone was keeping it a secret from me because Sober Teen Needs to Focus On Her Sobriety. But fuck that. Sober Teen Needs a Fucking Break. Sober Teen Needs a Little Fun.

You know how I learn about the Club 12 dances? From Grimace. The Deadhead with the toenails; you remember him, the guy from the Westport YP meeting. My mother finally lets me use the car again on a Saturday night, so I head back to that meeting because my booklet doesn't list a Saturday 8:30 PM at Club 12. And guess who's there? Grimace John *and* He-Man Aaron! When I walk in and see them, I want to, like, launch into a tap dance. Grant may hate me, but thank you, Jesus God, there are always other boys.

After the meeting, John says to me and Aaron, "You guys ever do the sober dances?"

I'm like, "Psychic friend! How'd you know about the tap dance?"

"The tap dance? No, I don't think they tap dance. But I dunno. I've never been."

"Yeah," Aaron says. "Not my scene either."

"What's not your scene? What are you guys talk—"

"The *sober* dances!" they both say at once, like, uh, *duhhh.*

"*What* sober dances? Like, the Hammer dance? The moonwalk?"

"What are you, stup—*God,*" Aaron goes. "The frigging *sober* dances. Dances where people with sobriety go. To dance. To mack on chicks. *Dances.*"

John's nodding his head, but at least he didn't start until after Aaron called me stupid.

"But...it's all *sober* people?" Maybe I am stupid. It's just, this is too good to be real. I can't even process it. "*Where?*"

"Oh, different places," John says. "But I know Club 12 has 'em every Saturday. You know Club 12, right?"

"Right *now*? At Club 12? Right up the road?"

"Right now. At Club 12. Right up the road."

"Oh my God, let's go! We're going! Come on!"

"No, nope, no way, no can do." That's both of them,

saying every possible version of no. My frigging luck. I get two sober guys—*two!*—but out of all the guys in the world, I get a surfer and a Deadhead, the two types least likely to go to a dance club. It even sounds like a joke: a surfer and a Deadhead walk into a sober dance...

Fuck them, though. Fuck them, and fuck Grant, and fuck Mary and Donna and the rest of the youth group, and fuck the popular kids and my mother and her boyfriends, and fuck *every*body. I'm going to the Club 12 sober dance. I don't care if I have to go alone. I don't even care if I have to steal my mother's car. I'm going where there's music and sobriety and dancing, where I don't have to see or worry about *any* of them. I'm going, and I'm dancing, and I'm forgetting every, fucking, thing, else.

I make that decision, and get a gift from God. I might not get friends or family, but I do get gifts sometimes. Because the very next Saturday night, my mother says I can use the car. She doesn't even pull a hostage scheme or make me sign my name in blood. She just says, "Okay. Put gas in it."

You can imagine how peppy I am, seven o'clock on Saturday night. I've got my outfit laid out on my bed—Indian skirt, silver anklet with bells, white tank top—and I shower, towel my hair, and put on a little Venetian Violet Flower Water.

And I smile, smile, smile as I head upstairs to my room, past my mother, who's sitting on the bottom stair, phone pressed to her ear. I smile, smile, smile as I clutch my towel tighter over my boobs, in case her latest boyfriend has X-ray phone vision. I smile, smile, smile till I hit the top stair, where my mother can look up from below and see everything under my towel. I stop there because that's what animals do, when we hear a scary noise. We freeze.

The noise is my mother's laughter. It floats up to me like arsenic bubbles.

"Ha! I've got a teenage daughter parading around in a towel here…"

I haul my ass out of there before I can hear what I know is coming next: "Want to come over?" There's this book we learned about in psych class: *My Mother, My Self*. I could write a new version: *My Mother, My Pimp*. If she says I can't use the car after all, I'm burning the house down. Swear to fucking God.

And God knows I'm not kidding, because He makes her leave me alone. Well, almost. Before I can leave, she clamps me in place, hands on my shoulders, and slow drags her gaze up and down my outfit.

"That's my skirt," she says, and my butt-stomach-throat cramp into a fist. She puts her hand too close to my z-z, picks up the skirt's belt, and flips it, to prove her point. But then God must remember I have those Sinclair's matches, because she says, "You look nice. Have fun."

And like a shot, I'm out the door. I spend the drive blaring the Milli Vanilli tape that Surfer Aaron lent me and trying to think up a way to make an outfit out of Dunkin' Donuts mugs. I would *so* walk around in a heavy plastic suit of DD armor, all orange, pink, and brown. I'd be, like, supernaturally protected.

Wait. A Dunkin' Donuts *suit*? What am I even talking about? See, no wonder the second I open my mouth, nobody likes me. I'm not talking to *any*one at this sober dance, 'cause I'm *not* fucking this up. This is my one chance to have a place to go where it's safe and fun and *cool*. This could be the greatest thing that ever happened to me. As long as I don't say a word, it *will* be.

I make it from the car to the dance, all alone, without a nervous breakdown. I've done this walk by myself a hundred times going to meetings, so it's normalish. Only diff is I have to stop in the doorway and hand over a fiver.

Then I step into the massive wood-floor room, the one you cross through to get to the meetings. And it's…salvation. It's rescue and redemption and absolution and sanctification. It's all those vocab words the Puritans were killing each other for in *The Crucible*. A few candy-colored lights cut the dark. People are dancing, instead of looking at each other. AA slogans are posted on the walls, like a safety net. And it's just-right loud, and it's Steve Winwood, and it's "Higher Love," which is a total program song. It's a love song to his recovery, to his higher power. To God. As soon as I step inside, I swear, the whole room starts singing along with him.

I melt into the crowd and I'm dancing and spinning and I feel hugged and lifted and part part part part of *this*. I have never felt so safe, so high, so loved, so part of a *group*. And it's perfect. And I know my higher power is here. And I have people here. And I'll be fine if I can just keep myself from opening my mouth.

It's gotta be three hours later when I finally take a break. I'm afraid I might look like I'm in a wet T-shirt contest from dancing so long and so hard, but it's okay. This is my place. These are my people. I go outside to breathe and look at stars, and I don't even need to cross my arms over my boobs to feel safe. I just walk through the people smoking and go down to the parking lot, so I'm not standing underneath the Club 12 spotlight.

And talk about gifts from God, there's a boy down there. An adorable boy. An adorable sober boy who came to a dance at Club 12. And he's got brown hair and a couple freckles and faded Levi's and an old gray T-shirt that says COLLEGE. He's the kind of perfect you'd never even dream of, because some shelves are just too high.

He's standing under a tree, tucked between two cars, smoking. I don't even realize he's there until I hear him speak: "Hey there." Just like that. "Hey there." He talked to *me*. I turn toward the "Hey there," but I made myself a promise, so I don't say a word. I just smile.

Neither of us moves and he says, "Sorry."

I'm still keeping my promise, so I look down.

He speaks again, like, "...for the smoke."

There's a million words in my head, laughing and singing and cartwheeling around like, "Oh my God, don't be sorry. I *love* the smell of smoke. I just don't *do* it. Smoke. My sobriety's not strong enough. But yours is, obviously. But I love the *smell* of cigarette smoke, which I think is okay, because it hasn't made me drink or drug yet, right?"

But I don't say a single one of them. I just half look up, half smile, and half shrug, all at once. And he—he *likes* it. You can tell. Because he keeps *looking* at me. In the good way. And then he drops his cigarette and smudges it out with his Top-Sider.

And he says to me, "I'm Shane."

It's like I'm the Arabian girl in the olden-days movies, with big eyes and a veil over her mouth. What can you *do* if you can't speak? You've got three choices: smile, look down, or walk away. I do everything but the last one, and Shane steps closer.

"Do you have a name?"

I smile instead of answer. I took a vow. This sober dance is Heaven, and I'm not ruining it. But Shane doesn't mind.

"Well, okay, shy girl. You don't like to talk. So how about this: I'll talk for you."

He leans back on a white Ford Fiesta, but his rear pockets are the only thing touching the car. His feet and head and shoulders are all pointing toward me, so his body's in the shape of the greater-than symbol. He's >. He pinches his chin with two fingers. Then, he talks.

"You live in Fairfield," he says, "in a white house with black shutters and a green lawn. You have two golden retrievers, but they don't have a doghouse, because they sleep inside, by the fire. How am I doing?"

I smile at my feet. I can feel him looking at my scalp, right where my eyes would be if I could lift my head to look back at him. He keeps talking for me.

"Your dad works in the city. He's a lawyer at a very important Manhattan firm. Your mother…your mother is an equestrian. Or is she a gardener? She gave up her Peace Corps plans when she met your father. It was a sacrifice, but she's resigned to her fate. She meets your dad in the city every Friday for dinner and a show. She's a Wellesley girl. He's a Princeton man."

I flick my eyes up for a split second and he's smiling at me. With his eyes, even. Like oh, my, oh my God, he likes me. He likes the me he's telling me about. It's the same feeling as if a butterfly lands on your hand: elation, because it chose *you*; plus terror, because if you even *breathe*, the miracle's over. That's me right now. Elation/terror. Terration. Elator.

I don't breathe. The miracle keeps going.

"And you," the miracle says, "you're a writer. You play field hockey because that's what Fairfield girls do. Even though you're three months sober, you still go to the beach keggers to keep your friends happy. But your heart's not in it. Your heart's in your journal with your purple ink pen. But Daddy's not having it. Daddy says you're going to law school, come hell or high water."

If Shane sees my hands, he'll know how far I am from being on the field hockey team. They're frigging shaking, my hands are. So I muzzle them with my butt. I lean back on the Mustang behind me, but I keep my feet, head, and shoulders facing him. I'm the lesser-than sign. I'm <.

"You're here tonight because your friends are on spring break, so your Saturday night is your own. And you don't have a curfew, because your parents are in Saint Bart's, even though it's *your* spring break. But you went on strike over the pre-law clash. An hour before the car arrived to take your family to JFK, you took your stand. You pulled out your finished Iowa Writers' Workshop application, complete with postage. I can hear your words, which is strange, since you won't let me hear your voice. You said, 'I'm *me*, Dad. Not you. I'm a writer, not a lawyer. You can't make me into what you wish I was!' And then you—what did you do next?"

Nobody's ever said so many words about me. Not in a row, and never ever so *nice*. It doesn't matter that the me he's describing is as fake as a Disney cartoon, because the guy telling the story *isn't* a cartoon. He's real as a Mack truck slamming into your car. Right as you hit exit 19.

"I know what you did. You picked up the phone and hit speed dial. And you said, 'Auntie Bronwyn?' while looking

Daddy in the eye. 'Can I stay with you this week? I don't feel like going to the islands again with Mummy and Daddy.' And that's how you won, and that's how *I* won. Because now, tonight, you're here. With me."

He leans forward, this freckled miracle, with his right hand extended toward me. I lean toward him and clap his palm with mine. They make that perfect pop, the one that tells all heaven and earth you've *got* it. You're cool. I've never gotten that pop from a high five before. I've maybe never even done a high five before. This not-talking thing, this is the fix for my life.

"They told me your face matched your name. You really do look like a Claire."

"What?" I say, pulling my hand away so he won't feel it shaking.

"Gotcha!" he says, leaning closer into me and grabbing my hand again. We look *right* at each other's eyes, and it feels like falling off a bridge and eating a hot fudge sundae and barfing out your nose, all at once. "I *knew* I'd get you to talk!"

He's right. I talked. I broke my promise to myself. It was just one syllable, but still. A slip is a slip. But what was he—

"Claire!" He drops my hand and leans back again, laughing. "Call a girl a Claire, and you're guaranteed a reaction. It's from *Breakfast Club*. John Bender said it: 'Claire is a fat girl's name.' Remember now? I'm totally kidding though. You're not a Claire."

But…he said my name went with my face. Who told him what? He thinks I'm someone else? That whole story was some *other* girl's? I can't even find out without talking more, so I'm fucked either way. So much for God's gifts.

"What's your name really?" he asks.

I have to make this work. This COLLEGE boy, he *likes* me. He said he's *winning* because I'm here! And it's all because of me not talking. But I can't be a mute freak when he asks me a question. What did the Arabian girl do in the movies? She danced. She fucking danced and stripped off her veils. Okay, never mind her. I'll talk, but only a *little* bit. Like one word at a time. That's *it*.

Ready? Go.

"Cyndy," I say.

"Cyndy, huh? That's more of a cheerleader name than a field hockey name, but it works. So Cyndy, how'd I do? I'm a writer myself, if you didn't guess. Fiction. So, do you live in Fairfield?"

"No."

"Okay, Westport?"

"No."

"Here? Southport?"

"No."

"Well, whatever. It doesn't matter where you live. How about…is your dad a lawyer?"

"Well, no." *One word answers! Fuck!*

117

"My dad, neither. But close enough. He's a politician. And a douche."

Perfect. Let him talk about *him*.

"Yeah?"

"Oh, yeah. Total. Know what kind of car he drives? A Porsche. See what kind of car *I* drive? *This*."

He knocks a knuckle on the Ford Fiesta, which looks like a dream mobile to me. It's shiny like it's brand new, for one thing, and it's gotta be *his*, not his parents', because there are stickers in the back windows. I step over to look at them, and guess what I see: dancing bears. Shane's a frigging Deadhead. He's also, like, a griffin. A mythical creature. How can he be cute and sober and rich *and* a Deadhead, and *still* be psyched to go to a dance on Saturday night? And if he's all of that, how can he like *me*?

"So, thanks for not laughing," he says.

"At?"

"At my car, man. Seriously. You weren't ripping on me in your head for this piece of shit, were you? It's my father's way of beating me. You know what I mean? He'd never lay an *actual* hand—who *does* that?—but he's gotta beat me *some*how, for draining his bank account and breathing his oxygen. I get back at him with the stickers."

The sticker on our side is one I've never seen before. It's the dancing bears kicking over a hill next to an ocean, surrounded by palm trees and sunbeams. The sticker on the other side is the classic: the big open skull with the lightning bolt through it.

"Deadhead?" I ask, but I say it so fast, it barely even counts as a word.

"God, shut *up*, wouldya? You talk too much. Yeah, I like the Dead, but more than that, I like knowing that *Councilman* Gallway gets his boxers in a twist every time I leave the house because his *constituents* are *perturbed* by my teddy bear stickers. Sometimes I park in front of Talbots for hours, just to see the old crones coming out make sour faces. The irony is they think my teddy bears mean I'm a drug dealer. But I'm here at a *sober* dance on Saturday night, while they're home pounding Glenlivet."

I laugh at that. More than one *ha*. But I guess it's okay, because Shane laughs too. And then he steps closer, which makes me really happy and really nervous. Nappy. Hervous.

"So," he says, from eight inches away from my face. "Did you like my fiction? Was I right about *any*thing?"

"Maybe."

"*May*be? What, your lawn *might* be green, but you can't tell because you're colorblind?"

"No, I—I'm a writer, maybe. I like to write." Too many words!

"Oh-ho! Nice!" he says, and claps his hands. *God*, is he cute. And maybe—maybe I didn't say too many words.

"We've got a writer, folks! Beautiful. Another word person. Well then. You'll like this."

"Like what?"

"Like Auntie Bronwyn. How wordy are you? Do you know what Bronwyn means?"

"Ummm...no?"

"I picked it just for you. It's a Welsh name. It means 'white, fair breast.'"

That safety feeling I had, because we're at Club 12? Gone. I try to look down at my feet, but my boobs, in their wet, white tank top, are in the way. I hug my arms over them and don't say anything. For once, I can't think of anything to say.

I have a boyfriend! And it's Shane! I don't even know who I *am* anymore, swear to God. You know how when people temporarily die, they hover over their hospital bed and watch as their body gets operated on? That's how I feel right now. The real Cyndy Etler—the loser, the Straightling—is up above watching this skinny, quiet girl who's using my name and wearing my hair.

My sponsor makes me feel like the real me, though, when I call to tell her about Shane. She takes the flare right out of my fireworks, cutting me off with, "I don't think you're ready." She uses the doomsday tone, the farthest left key on the piano. I let her reel off all the reasons that my three and a half years of sobriety aren't enough to qualify me as "ready to date." Then, when she stops talking, I say, "Okay, Suzanne. Gotta go," and hang up.

It's a kind of ballsy move because I *never* don't say "you're right" when someone disagrees with me. I *always* roll with what other people say. The one time I didn't? My mother's husband beat me up, and my mother just watched, so I ran away. Which got me locked up in Straight for sixteen months. Yeah, bad idea, Cyndy making her own decisions. *Bad* idea. But maybe this new, quiet, skinny Cyndy is gonna mix it up. Maybe she'll be the badass that original Cyndy can't muster the balls for.

Masuk High School, though. Masuk is new-Cyndy Kryptonite. As soon as I enter that school, I'm the loser version of myself. It doesn't matter that I've got on Guess jeans, or that four different sober guys have talked to me, or that the last time I got on my mother's scale, it said frigging 117. Doesn't matter. The Masuk kids know the original me, and they're not changing their minds. I'm like a double agent: teen loser by day, teen hottie by night.

The only exceptions are Jack and Whitney. They break that rule and see the new me. Like the other day. The band teacher was out, and Mr. Littberger said we could mess around with the boom box and play whatever we wanted. So Jack—who plays the drums, by the way, did I tell you that? He's *so* frigging cool—puts in this tape and yells, "Everybody? Assume the position! Let's do the Time Warp again!" And like, nine-tenths of the kids in band get up and they—well, they dance. And sing. And like, hump the air in front of them. It's in*sane*. And *awesome*. But I have no idea what it *is*.

In English class, I pass Jack a note that says, "What *was* that? (~in band~)" and he writes back and says, with a zillion squiggles and exclamation points all around it, "The Time Warp! It will be time again at 12 midnight on Saturday. Meet us!" and he puts an address for a movie theater in Milford. You better believe that note is pinned to my corkboard, so I see it every day.

So I have not one, but *two* killer options for tonight. Like I said, who *am* I? But there's really no question when one of the options is to go to your rich boyfriend's house when his parents aren't home.

Shane lives in a town called Weston, which I never knew existed. It's so rich and green and isolated, it doesn't get named on highway signs. I drive around twisty roads with no streetlights for an hour before I find his house.

Shane meets me in his driveway in bare feet. For some reason, that feels like a bad sign. We go through the garage— "Where the Porsche lives, when it's home"—and into a room with a fireplace, a TV, an armchair, and a sofa. And we stop. He plops down in the armchair and picks up the TV remote and I stand there, feeling slapped. *This* is my first date with my rich boyfriend? Standing next to his armchair like a scullery maid?

He switches the channel from Nickelodeon to MTV, which is playing that White Lion song "When the Children Cry." The black-and-white video jumps from a guy with big hair and tights spinning on a stage to an empty swing set at night, which is international code for Something Really Bad Happened. I can't just stand there, so I sit on the edge of a sofa cushion and try to look fascinated with the video.

Shane makes a sound like he's trying to clear a hairball. "*This* shit!" he says, shaking the remote at the TV. "Are you a metal singer or a soothsayer? I won't even start on the mantyhose with cowboy boots." Then he looks at me. "Why do chicks dig these faggots?"

I stick with my plan of very few words. "Well, 'faggots'? I don't think—"

"Never mind," he says. He points the remote and clicks it, hard, to VH1.

It's another black-and-white vid, but this one's Paula Abdul. "Straight Up." She gives the whole room a blood transfusion. The night feels suddenly happy and, just, *possible*. I know how fucking stupid this is, but I almost feel like dancing.

Before I can stop myself I go, "I love this song! Turn it up!"

Shane gives himself whiplash turning to look at me. "You *what*? That's it. Get out," he says, jumping up and beelining to the door to the garage. Really. He does this in his bare feet, holey jeans, and untucked Polo shirt. He's lord and

124

master of his domain, looking at me like I'm the dog shit that made him leave his shoes outside.

Like all dog shit, I can't move. I'm hot with shame but frozen in place. How could I be so *stupid* as to think I could be my real self in a Weston house? And what do I do now? Is he serious? Am I supposed to leave?

"Ahhh! Just joshin'," he says, and strides over to sit next to me on the sofa. "Your face! You should've seen your face! It went through every color in the Crayola box."

He clicks back to Nickelodeon, which is playing *You Can't Do That on Television*. The girl with the hair like mine goes, "I don't know," and gets slimed. The cool, thick sludge that gets dumped on her is like her own personal gift from God. Now nobody can see what her face is doing or what color she's turning.

Shane picks up my hand from my lap and curls his fingers through mine. So, okay. Maybe I'm okay. Maybe he still likes me.

He turns his face toward me and tilts it like a listening dog. Like we just shared a Hallmark moment. "You know I was kidding, right? You just gotta understand: I *hate* Paula Abdul. Every dude *hates* Paula Abdul. Remember that."

Then he leans in and kisses me. I fuck you not. He kisses me. Me, the pile of dog shit. Getting kissed. By a rich Weston politician's son. And just like that, I'm *in* again.

The kiss is no Turkish Delight. It's more like the porridge

those Narnia kids ate for breakfast. But maybe that's because of where the kiss is happening. Maybe leaning on a car under the stars with I-95 rushing past makes for a better kiss. Maybe kissing in a brown living room in a house you didn't get a tour of makes for a dog-shit kind of kiss.

But things can happen fast in houses. Especially when the mom and dad aren't home.

I wait till he stops kissing me to ask, "Who's here?"

He smiles like I told him a secret and says, "Just my brother. But he's down in the basement rec room playing Nintendo."

I think, *Just your brother?*

I say, "You have a rec room?"

"Yeah. It's lame. I'd show you around if we were at the Hampton's house. It's way nicer. This house? There's nothing worth seeing."

If I were being the real me I'd say, "What're you *talking* about, nothing to see? You have a house with a mom and a dad and a brother and cable TV. And Nintendo and your own car and probably even Softsoap and Pop-Tarts and a dishwasher that works."

Instead I say, "Oh."

He leans in like he's gonna kiss me again, but all I can think is, what's gonna happen *next*, with nobody home but his brother? So I lean back and say, "Do you have a bathroom?"

"No," he says. "Sorry. You're gonna have to use the spit can out back. Duh, do we have a bathroom? Come on."

He stands and pulls me up with a tug, then swoops his arm out to square-dance-swing me around the sofa and into a doorway. Which is the kind of thing Grant would do. Which is the kind of boyfriend-y stuff I've always dreamed of.

But wait. This *is* my boyfriend. He asked me out, officially, on the phone Wednesday night. I *have* to let him kiss me. That's what girlfriends do.

When I come out of the bathroom, he's lying on the sofa, propped up on his elbow. He's patting the cushion in front of him. He "wants" me, which should make me feel great. Instead, it makes me want to sit in his armchair and pick up his remote. Or dig through his mom's kitchen cabinets. Or go look for that spit can out back.

"C'mere!" Shane says, patting the cushion again.

On my bulletin board, next to Jack Pilgrim's note from class, I have a note from Shane. He didn't write it to me, though. It was on his passenger seat one night when we were standing outside Club 12. He told me the story about it and said I could keep it. He wrote the note in red Magic Marker to the girls in the car next to his on the highway.

He and his friends had been driving back from skiing in Vermont. And this girl driver, Shane said, had been totally matching his speed for miles. Her friends were trying to talk to Shane's friends through the windows with sign language.

It wasn't working. So Shane had his buddy hold the steering wheel while he wrote the note and held it up to the girls.

GANG BANG?

The girls drove away. Which I don't get. If cute boys who have their own car are saying they like you, how do you drive away?!

Those girls are what I'm thinking about as I sit on the sofa by Shane's feet. They drove away, so they didn't get a boyfriend. I got him instead. A real live, sober, Weston boyfriend. For me. Cyndy Etler. It's impossible, but it's true. Shane is sitting up. He's leaning in. He's kissing me. We're kissing.

I'm positive I'm doing it wrong. Rich kids know how to do this stuff, but I am *so* far from rich. Oh my God, do I not belong here.

Shane pulls me down onto the sofa with him. I don't feel good nervous, the way I did with Grant. I feel scared nervous. Shane's about to tell me, "You suck at this." Shane's about to say, "Get out," and mean it this time.

We're lying down. We're kissing. Shane's breathing hard through his nose, like a bull.

He tries to put a hand up my shirt, and I block him with the boney part of my arm, between my wrist and elbow. He tries to put a hand on my waistband, and I hip jerk away. When I was in Straight, I had to say I was a druggie whore. But I'm not. I'm not.

Shane grabs my wrist and pushes my hand at his crotch. It takes every muscle I have to whip my hand away.

He moves his lips from my mouth to my ear and says, "If you don't make me cum, I'm gonna rape you."

If I could breathe, maybe I'd say the words in my head: "But I don't know how."

Shane's brother picks that moment to come up from the basement. God, maybe *he's* the one I love. Shane goes to the bathroom and stays there a long, long time.

I can see her through the giant front window as I'm trudging up the driveway after school—my mother. First thought: *Fuck, there goes my nap.* Second: *Hey, maybe she'll let me take the car!* Third: *Wait, why is she* home? Then I get closer to the window. Fourth: *Fuck, what the* fuck?

My mother's sitting at the kitchen table, staring at nothing. Her mascara is in *Clockwork Orange* streaks down her face.

I can't carry this. Whatever it is, it's too heavy. I can't even try to sneak in the back door, because I'm the one who locked it. You've got to keep doors locked when there's an ex-stepfather around.

She doesn't look up when I walk by the window, when I push open the front door. She doesn't immediately start talking about herself. That's the red-hot warning: her silence.

"Hey," I say. I drop my bag so hard it makes an earthquake. Still, she doesn't move. "What are you doing here?" Not even a sniff. "Are you okay?" That's her dinner bell. If she doesn't accept an invitation to complain, she's got no pulse.

Nothing.

"Ma. What's wrong?" I put my face at a weird sideways angle, to force her eyes to see mine. That works. She blinks.

"He touches her."

"What?"

"Your sister. She told me. I was changing her diaper before daycare. She told me."

"Told you *what?*"

"She wasn't crying. She was just talking. She was fine. She just...*said* it."

"Said *what?*"

I see it coming up, her puke. It moves like an elevator. It's a bump, then a blast, from her chest to her throat to her cheeks. Her eyes bulge and she closes her mouth on the gag.

She does me that one favor: she doesn't puke on me. She swallows, instead. For my mother, this is a gift. I move my head away from her. I can't be looking at her eyes for whatever she says next.

"She said, 'When—'" My mother gets that far, and I need to fucking bolt. I don't want her puke, I don't want her stare, and I really don't want her words. But she beats me. She says it before I can jet. "'—when Daddy changes my diaper, he touches my z-z.'"

Then I do. I run. I run like greased lightning. I run out the door and down the driveway and I fall and rip my knees, but I push up and I run and run and run. And it hurts, and thank God, because the hurt is in my knees, my lungs, my sides, but not my z-z. It's not in my z-z. I run until I reach the woods, and then I fall and stay there.

It takes me hours to get back home, because I'm carrying this weight. It's too heavy. I have to put it down.

I call my boyfriend. I call Shane.

"Hey, I gotta… Can you come pick me up? I gotta get out of here. I can't take this."

"Take what? You can come down here. My parents aren't home. Get your mother's car."

"I can't. She's not talking. I can't talk to her. Can you—"

"Waddaya mean, 'She's not talking'? Don't be stupid. Use your words. 'Mother, I'm borrowing your car. Please and thank you.' *Capisce?*"

"No, you don't—you don't understand."

"I can understand anything but you not coming to my house when my parents are out. Hit me."

"No seriously, you don't—"

"Hit me. Get it out, so we can move on and get you getting your ass down to Weston."

"Shane, I promise. You don't want to—"

"Tell me, or I'm breaking up with you."

"Mybabysistertoldmymotherherfathertouchesher."

"..."

"When he changes her diaper."

"..."

"I know. I know! I can't—I *told* you!"

"But...that doesn't mean anything."

"What?"

"How old is she? She's in *diapers*? That's not even possible. Just because she said that doesn't mean it happened."

"No, you don't—it's not just *her*. It happened to—"

"I gotta go. My brother's calling. B—"

click

Okay, I'll call my sponsor. I'll just call my sponsor. I'll break my rule and tell her about my real life. She'll understand, because this is an emergency.

I'll tell her what happened last time my sister went for visitation. How I overheard my mother teaching my sister a lesson. How my mother was brushing my sister's hair and talking about me. I'll tell my sponsor, and she'll understand. She'll get it. She'll tell me I'm not going crazy.

We had just had a fight, and my mother was pissed. I guess she needed my sister to be pissed at me too. I walked by the door to her room and heard, "Your sister *Cyndy* is a *drug* addict. She's a bad, bad girl. She had to go away to a jail, to make her stop taking drugs. But you're a *good* girl, aren't you?"

My sister didn't react. I don't even know if she understood. I held my breath to hear what else my mother would say, but she was quiet. She finished brushing my sister's hair, put her in the car, and delivered her to my ex-stepfather's house.

I don't know why, but I have to tell somebody. About my sister. How she didn't say anything, like, "I don't want to go." How she just got in the car and *went*, when my mother told her to. How she had no choice.

I call my sponsor, and her mother answers. She calls out her name—*Suza-annne!*—in a voice like a silver bell. She must have set the phone down with the receiver facing up, because I can totally hear what's happening in their clean, rich house. There's classical music going, and more than one person is talking at once. Somebody laughs. Then I hear the cottony **Kz-shwp!** of the phone being picked back up.

"Hello?" Suzanne asks.

"Hi…it's me."

"Cyndy? Hi… Hang on." Then a shorter **Kz-shwp**, and she's talking to someone with her hand over the mouthpiece. Then she's back. "Hi, sorry. What's going on? I've got people over, so…"

I can practically feel the room she's in—what it smells like, how the light looks. Books on shelves, board games stacked, family friends helping her mom make dinner. Suzanne has the life that skipped me when my father died.

"I'm sorry," I say. "I don't want to bother you. But something happened. I really need to talk about it."

"Can it wait? Like I said, I've got company."

"I know. I'm sorry. I just I feel like—"

Somebody laughs near the phone; Suzanne goes *shh!*

"Here, let me take this phone somewhere quieter," she says. It's a total verbal hug. There's a clunk and then quiet. She must be in her dad's library.

"Thank you. I'm so sorry. It's just, I got home from school today, and—"

"Cyndy, listen. I have to stop you."

"What?"

"I'm sorry. But I can't do this. I can't be your sponsor. It's too much."

I can't hear the ticking of the grandfather clock, but I may as well. It's counting the seconds till I collapse in a pile of rubble, like those short black-and-white films of a skyscraper getting dynamited.

"Cyndy, are you there? I'm sorry, but I—" she says, before a voice calls out from the background, "*Suze! Come on!*"

"I'm so sorry, Cyndy. You'll be okay without me. There're way better sponsors out there."

Tick-tick-tick.

"So—*Suze! Dinner!*—so I'll see you at the club, k?"

BOOM.

At first I was saving this outfit for when Grant asked me on a date. Then I was saving it for when Shanc wanted to go somewhere other than his house. But now I'm sick of waiting, so fuck it. I'm gonna wear my date outfit today: brown silk pants, black angora sweater, and black suede pumps. When Japanese boyfriend weirdly gave me a business suit, the Macy's tags were still on it. I just traded the suit for these fancy, New Yorkish clothes. I'm a little sad about giving up my dream of having an actual *date,* but I really need a pick me up today.

I spent ten months on first phase in Straight. Ten months with an oldcomer watching me shit, with an oldcomer gripping the back of my pants, steering me around every time I stood up. I, like, *really* wanted to get off first phase. But to do that, I had to confess every single incident from my past to my mother. I had to admit that every bad thing, ever, was 100 percent my fault. So that's what I did. Every time I earned a five-minute talk with my mother, I told her the details of every ugly, scary, thrilling, risky moment of my life. And then I confessed it was all my fault. But outside of those talks, we've *never* discussed what happens in this house. God. Why would we?

Today, though. I don't know. I feel a little crazy. There's something itching my brain, and I have to get it out. This itchy thought is saying, maybe it *wasn't* all my fault. Maybe someone *else* was the bad guy.

When I shuffle downstairs for coffee, my mother is at the kitchen table, reading the back of a cereal box. An invisible *Do Not Disturb* sign flashes over her head. But I can't help it. The words are out before I can lock them back in their vault.

"Ma, do you remember Jacque, like, hitting me and stuff? When I was little?"

For a second, I don't think she heard me. She sips her coffee and keeps her eyes on the Honey Bunches of Oats.

"Ma?"

"I don't remember that at all, Cyndy. But anything he may have done to you, you deserved it. You brought it on yourself. You were a *very* difficult child."

I go back upstairs to put my outfit on, because fuck coffee.

My brain is still itchy. It's crazy itchy, on-fire itchy, like it's crawling with fucking head lice. I'm walking down the hall between first and second period, trying to balance both my heels and my brain. Nobody teaches you how to walk in high heels; you're supposed to just *know*. And nobody teaches you how to deal with your mother; you're supposed to just *deal*. But I can't. I can't deal. I keep hearing her in my head, on repeat. "You deserved it. You deserved it. You brought in on yourself."

I know I don't look right, because kids are staring. My date outfit isn't hiding shit. Plus, I don't have my Dunkin' mug to shield me. These kids in the hallway, they see it all. They see my brain lice, crawling and burning. They see Shane hanging up on me and Suzanne kicking me to the curb. They see Jacque touching me and my mother watching and kids spitting in my face at Straight. I don't know how they see it, but they do. I can tell by how they're looking at me. They all know all about me.

It's too much to balance, the itch and the heels and the diapers and the words. I have to scratch it all out. I have to get to a stall and dig my nails in and scratch it all out of my brain. Have to get away from all these eyes. Have to get to a bathroom with a door that closes so I can—**schwink**. I fucking slip on my fucking high heel. I stumble, I don't fall, but the cheerleaders—I hear them. They're always fucking there. Always fucking laughing.

I take off my pumps and tear down that hallway, past the social studies rooms, past Mrs. Skinner's room, out that side door nobody ever uses. And I sit—I fucking fall—onto the grass as the **DING-DING-DING** period two bell goes off. Then silence. All the happy students are tucked safe in their classrooms, clearheaded and eager to learn, as I sit here in a crumple and need to die. Need. I need to be done.

I already know how. It's totally easy. Middle of the night. Car keys. Garage doors down. Ignition on. Sleep. Done. Bye.

Tonight. Tonight I'll do it. And finally, finally, I'll be fucking safe.

Mrs. Skinner is getting her second-block English class going. I can hear her because I'm right underneath her open window. She's reading aloud. *Catcher in the Rye.* Thank fucking *God* nobody is out here, because all of a sudden I'm sobbing. She's reading in her excellent voice, and she's making it all make sense. He's desperate, the narrator. He sees everything; he *gets* everything. Too much. He gets it all way too much. He loves people, but they can't love him back. Because all they have is pain. That's all they have to give. Everywhere he goes, someone's graffitied "fuck you," and he can't take it. He can't carry everyone's pain anymore.

But then there's the donuts. He orders coffee and donuts, but he can't eat. So the waiter takes the donuts away and doesn't charge him. That little niceness. Like, thirty cents.

The waiter was nice. He didn't have to be, but he was. That's what grabs me and shakes.

There's a counselor. In the guidance office. She said I could talk to her.

But I can't go back in that school. I can't go back to my house. I can't *do* this anymore.

But the waiter was nice. The counselor is nice. Bitsy is nice. Connie is nice. Mrs. Skinner is nice. I'm nice. There is nice. Maybe there's not as much nice as pain, but nice is out there. Maybe I could try to find it. Like a treasure hunt.

I have to decide. I'm either going to kill myself, or I'm going into that school and finding that counselor. One or the other. Which is stronger, the nice or the pain? Which one?

Ms. Grass, the school counselor, is on hold a long, long time while the nursing home receptionist goes to find my mother. We sit and stare at the information card on Ms. Grass's desk. She taps a finger on the typewritten words PARENT WORK PHONE, highlighted in yellow.

Ms. Grass hugged me when I told her I wanted to die. I think she believed me.

When my mother picks up, she's so loud that I can hear both sides of the conversation. She's using her mad voice.

"Recreation Therapy, this is Nadine," she says.

"Mrs. Etler, hello. This is Ms. Grass, calling you from

Masuk High School Guidance. I've got your daughter Cyndy here with me."

"Of course you do. It's always something. What is she saying today?"

"Mrs. Etler, you need to take your daughter to see someone who can help her. Someone who she can talk to, who can prescribe medication. Sooner is better than later."

"*She* needs help! Do you know what she's done to me? Do you know we had to pull her out of your school and send her to a tough-love facility? She's a *druggie*. She's put me through—"

"Mrs. Etler. Mrs. *Et*ler. I'm sorry to say this to you over the phone—" Ms. Grass looks at me with eyes as kind as the Jesus illustrations in a kids' Bible. Then she turns away and scoops her hand around the phone and her mouth. I hear her anyway. "Your daughter is suicidal. Deeply. She needs to be taken to a psychiatrist, *today*. I can give you a few names and—"

"A psychiatrist? Fancy! Do you think I can afford that? You must think—"

"You *have* to afford that, Mrs. Etler. Or, rather, you have a choice. You can pay for a psychiatrist or you can pay for a funeral."

I push my fingertips in my ears and tiptoe out of that office, but I don't go farther than the waiting area. I want Ms. Grass to know I didn't run away. College brochures are spread across the table like appetizers, shiny with pictures of safe, smiling kids in university sweatshirts. They're holding suitcases and waving goodbye to their parents. I shuffle them around a little, looking for a sign. If I find a Smith College brochure, that'll be my answer.

There's no Smith.

Instead of writing "fuck you" on the wall of the guidance waiting area, I do a bubble-letter **?**. In the empty middle part of the **?**, I write a poem-thing.

> A tisket
> A tasket
> Smith College
> or
> A casket

Then I draw little question marks around the main one, like falling snow. Like a question storm.

Shane hasn't called me since I told him about my little sister, but that's okay. It's okay! It's okay because of Prozac. The psychiatrist said I needed a double dosage, eighty milli-somethings a day. She said she'd never seen a teenager as depressed as I was. But *was*. Past tense. The psychiatrist said it can take a month for Prozac to kick in, but not for me! The first *day* I took my Prozac, I didn't need to go to my room and cry for two hours when I got home from school. It was unbelievable.

And, and, and! Speaking of unbelievable, there's another sober kid at Masuk now! I swear, sometimes I have to suffer awhile to prove something to God. Once I've proved it, He gives me everything I've ever wanted.

Ms. Grass really knows what she's doing, 'cause here's how she introduces us. She sends me a pass fifteen minutes into first period, when there's nobody left in the hallways. That way I don't have to walk by the cheerleaders in the popular zone. When I get to her office, she says to me, "There's someone I'd like you to meet." Then she walks me down the silent, empty halls until we reach the one single person who's not in class. It's this girl, standing in front of an open locker.

I swear, it's like the two halves of a couple meeting for their arranged marriage. Except in our case, we instantly fall in like, rather than love.

Her name's Deanna Fazzini, and she thinks she went to rehab. I'd never tell her this, but she didn't go to rehab. She went to preschool. First of all, she was only gone for six weeks. Which she thinks is a long time! Second, *she had her own private bathroom. With a door. That locked.* Third, she was allowed to read and go outside and be alone and choose her own food in a cafeteria. And nobody ever laid a hand on her. Like, the kids in her rehab went into frigging town on Saturday nights to see a movie!

The only rehabby thing about her program was that she wasn't around her druggie friends. Well, and she went to AA meetings three times a day. Other than that, the place was actually nice to her. How's *that* gonna help a lying, druggie scumbag kick her addiction? But somehow it seems to be working. At least, it's working so far. She's been out a month, and she hasn't talked to any of her druggie friends, and she hasn't picked up a drink or a drug. I've even seen her smile. One month out, and already she can smile. I've been out two years, and I *still* don't think I've smiled yet.

Deanna came back to Masuk at the perfect time, because, *man*, did I need a friend. So here's Deanna Fazzini. My first sober friend.

She's five-foot-two, and she thinks she's fat. Which is crazy. She wears a size six.

She's got long, straight brown hair that she blow-dries. Her bangs are curled in roll, so there's a huge bang-wave over her forehead. Her hair is really crispy because she uses a ton of hairspray. Aussie brand.

She has a cat face, like Paula Abdul, who's her idol. She does her eyes the same way as Paula—lots of eyeliner, not a lot else. And she always, always, always has on lipstick.

She wears the same outfit every day, only with different clothes: acid-wash jeans rolled up tight at the ankles. A brown leather belt. And a tight cotton ballerina shirt, the kind you can pull down off your shoulders if you want, which Deanna does. Plus sneakers—clean white Keds. And a heart locket with no picture in it, and some big hoop earrings.

Sometimes she'll trade the leotard shirt for a giant Reebok sweatshirt, the collar and wristbands removed, so the hem rolls a little to show the soft, nubbly inside. I think she wears that when she's bloated. Sweatshirt days, she trades the Keds for Velcro high-top Reeboks, like Jane Fonda wears in her exercise videos.

Deanna's "rehab" was in Minnesota, so she uses weird Minnesota slang. She calls soda "pop" and she cuts "come with me" down to "come with." That's how I knew we were immediate friends. After Ms. Glass introduced us and walked away, Deanna slammed her locker and said to me, "I'm going to the smoking pit. Wanna come with?"

Aside from finally, finally having a friend at Masuk—any sober friend, period!—the absolute best thing about Deanna is her home life. I've always known some kids live like her, but none of those kids ever liked me before. So being friends with Deanna is my first time actually getting to taste it, you know? Richness.

Listen to how she lives. First off, she has a mom *and* a dad. They're so *mom and dad* that mom doesn't have to work, and dad wears a tie every day. They're so *mom and dad* they let me call them Mom and Dad Fazzini.

!!!

They have one of those perfect houses that's all new and clean, with the same number of windows to the left and right side of the front door, and no missing shutters. They have TVs in the family room *and* in Mom and Dad Fazzini's room *and* in Deanna's brother's room, and all of the TVs have remote controls and cable. You could live all day, every day, *never* having to think with that much cable TV.

And Deanna's room! It's Shangri-fucking-La. Listen to me.

- Bedroom set—heavy, square, dark, wooden. Dresser, bed, nightstands, *dressing* table.
- Stereo. Not boom box. *Stereo.* Radio, tape deck, record player. Four speakers, each three feet tall.
- Chinese lanterns. Purple, pink, and turquoise.
- Blinds *and* curtains, which match the bedspread.
- Pillows. A zillion of them. Tubes, circles, hearts, plus regular rectangular sleeping pillows.
- Department store perfumes. One with the puffer-on-a-cord-and-a-tassel thing. On a silver tray.
- Hamper. Her own individual hamper. Which Mom Fazzini cleans out for laundry day.
- Door with a lock. And key. Which Deanna gets to keep all for herself.
- Closet so packed with clothes from Express/Contempo Casuals/Wet Seal, the hangers won't budge. And heels. Six pairs. Real spike heels. Not pumps.

This isn't her dream; she *lives* here.

And when she leaves here—which why *would* she, but when she does—she leaves *in her own Oldsmobile.* Swear to fucking God. She has her own cush car with velvet seats that goes click *vroom* like a lullaby when she turns the key. She can roll down the windows, tap in a Richard Marx tape, and drive, drive, drive, with me in the front seat next to her like a real live friend. She doesn't even bat an eyelash.

She only listens to Richard Marx when I'm in the car, because other than Paula Abdul, he's the only non-headbanger she likes. I can't handle being trapped in a car with a blaring metal band, which is the music she really loves. You can kind of tell that she'd be into Slayer and Poison and Whitesnake by looking at her. It's something about how she holds her mouth. She automatically looks a little mad if you don't know her. But she's not. She's actually nice—obviously, if she switches to Richard Marx for me.

Okay, confession? The whole hair band thing is maybe a little embarrassing. I mean, I'm a Dead-shirt person. The people who I want to, like, *respect* me are the Deadheads. So how does it look when I'm leaning my head in to whisper with Deanna, the black-shirted hairspray chick? But rewind. Erase. I can't believe I complained about my friend, now that I finally *have* one. God. I just wish she didn't have to be so loud about making fun of dancing bears and patchouli when we're in the smoking pit. You know?

Once we're away from the Deadheads, though, it doesn't matter. When it's just Deanna and me, it feels like we're the best friends in a *Seventeen* magazine fashion spread. The kind who talk with only their eyes, share clothes, and go on midnight field trips to the swings at the elementary school. Except our magazine-life is even better because it's the clean and sober version.

For example, a couple weeks ago, I saw this great picture

of Madonna in *Tiger Beat*. She was lying on a bed in an undershirt and boxer undies. I loved it. I showed it to Deanna and she loved it too. So we pooled our money and went to Kmart and bought a three-pack of Fruit of the Loom boxers. We tried them on with some of her dad's undershirts, and once we safety-pinned the fly shut, they made the cutest shorts. For the first time in my life, I looked in the mirror and saw a non-loser.

So I have been trying to get Deanna to try a Trumbull meeting—she doesn't seem to like AA much; I don't know why—and our matching outfits finally do the trick. The Friday night meeting is the perfect opportunity to wear them, even Dee can see that. Especially when I tell her some hot older guys show up at that meeting.

When I first got out of Straight and came to Trumbull meetings by myself, I would always share. I guess I had a lot to talk about back then. But Deanna doesn't speak at Friday's meeting, and neither do I. And then she wants to jet right after, to go to the diner. When we walk through the smoking crew on the way back to her car, I can feel some of my old AA people looking at me in the not-happy way. Like maybe they wish I weren't wearing underwear out in public. Which makes me kind of sad. But not sad enough to not feel awesome when Deanna slides down the windows, cranks up "Fight For Your Right," and burns rubber out of the church parking lot.

22

I think Deanna likes…sex. I don't know if she's actually *done* it, but I think she might have. I know she knows stuff about it. One day, we're actually hanging out at my house, and when we're in the bathroom trying on makeup, she sees my birth control pill case.

"Oh, you've done it?" she says, all casual, no big. She makes that hard *O* you do with your lips when you're putting on lipstick and looks at me in the mirror.

"No! No! Have you?!"

Instead of answering me, she runs her shoplifted Wet 'n' Wild Lip Tricks around the *O*. "So cool," she says. "How does it go from green in the tube to red on your lips?" She hands it over to me. "You try."

On me, it turns cotton candy pink. That's the end of our sex talk that day. But the next night, we pick it up again.

I'm staying over her house, and it's 2:00 a.m. We've got the family room TV on super-low, to not wake up her parents. When the video for that song "Luka," the one about a kid who gets beaten, comes on, we both get silent. I cry a little, and I know Deanna does too, because she has to blow her nose. Then they play another tearjerker, "Fast Car." So we're flat-out bawling, which means some honesty is going to happen. Next thing you know, when "I Want Your Sex" comes on, we're talking about our deepest fears. Or I guess *I'm* talking about my deepest fears, and Deanna's telling me how to fix them.

Q: What if he wants to kiss you but you haven't brushed your teeth since that morning?

A: Binaca. Keep it, always, in your back pocket.

Q: What if he tries to put your hand on his thing?

A: Over the jeans: make a fist and press *gently* up and down against it—but *not* on top of the zipper! Not, not, not! Under the jeans: same deal, just be careful because he's gonna try to get it *in* your hand, then *in* other places.

Q: Do I *want* my hand on his thing?

A: Long look, short shrug, then words: "That's something you've gotta figure out for yourself."

Q: What does the thing *feel* like?

A: A bumpy, clammy hot dog.

152

To get away from that topic, I tell her about my boob sweat. She laughs, so I go into more detail. "Look! Look at these things! These are big! And they get all smashed together in this stupid underwire bra. Big plus smashed plus bouncing around all day? Sweat! And sweat equals stink! What if a boy is kissing me and my sweat stink rises up to his nose, like the smell of baking cookies? What if he tries to put his *face* down there? Gas mask!"

She's literally crying from laughing now, and so am I. When we finally switch to eye wiping and wheezing, we hear this **swip** from the kitchen. We freeze. We listen. Nothing, nothing, **swip**.

I'm totally holding my breath. I look at her and she looks at me and we do that *Seventeen*-mag-best-friends trick: we talk with no words. I raise my brows and jerk my thumb at the kitchen. She frowns and nods twice for *yup*. I clench my teeth and peel my lips back like *yiiiikes*. Then I mouth, *Dad?* and she yup-nods again.

I crash my head down and knot my arms over it because oh my fucking GOD, her dad knows that my boobs stink, and why is he up reading the *news*paper at 2:00 a.m., and why didn't he *tell* us he was there? Between my bent knees, I can see that Deanna is *shaking* from trying to muzzle her laugh. I am mor-ti-fied. How can I ever call him "Dad" again?

But at the same time, I'm the happiest I've ever been in my life. Because I think have a friend. Like, a *best* friend.

I *know* I do when she agrees to go to a sober dance. Like I said, Deanna's not a fan of the AA scene. But we're going to Club 12 tonight, basically because *I* want to. Like, wait. What?

Yeah. Really.

So remember how, in *Desperately Seeking Susan*, loser housewife Roberta transforms herself into mega-hot Susan by putting on Susan-style clothes? I swear I'm her as we go through Deanna's closet and I try on her clothes. It's stuff I would never ever, ever think to wear, because it's all stretchy and tight.

We both end up looking like we're on MTV. She's Samantha Fox in a denim miniskirt and white ballerina top, with high-heel ankle boots and a giant cross necklace. She does her hair same as always, but she puts on extra makeup: dark-maroon blusher so her cheeks look all hollow, purple lipstick, and mascara, mascara, mascara.

I'm one of the "Addicted to Love" video chicks, minus the guitar and the oiled-back hair. I'm wearing Deanna's favorite baby-sized spandex mini, which is even shorter on me than her, since I'm two inches taller. She makes me try it on with these super-skinny high-heeled sandals and a spaghetti-strap tank top, then she piles my hair on my head all messy. When I look in the mirror I gasp, sort of, because who *is* that person? That person's not me. That person is— that person is, like, *sexy*.

But there's no way I'm going out in public with my big

boobs in spaghetti straps. So I wear my own long-sleeve black T-shirt. I do keep the heels on, though, and I let Deanna put makeup on me. And I look good. I look *good*.

When we're at Club 12, I can't imagine why anyone would need drugs ever, because with these outfits and this music and having an actual friend, I am higher than the birds, than the stars, than even God Himself. I am high on Club 12 and this night and "Mercedes Boy," which is what the DJ plays the second we walk in the door. The song starts out with this drum and guitar sound that feels threatening, somehow. Dangerous. The drum lands right between your hips. I don't even put my purse down. I don't care if I'm pushing through people or if Deanna is coming with; I'm *getting* to the middle of that dance floor and moving the way the music tells me.

Right before the singing, when those heaven-voice *tahhh-tah-tahhh*s go high to low, the singer, Pebbles takes over my body. I'm doing the same moves she does in the video, spreading my fingers across my face and moving them to my chest and middle, looking down in shock like Cinderella realizing, "Oh my God, I've got this beautiful dress on!"

I'm gone. I'm someone else, somewhere else, where everything feels good and easy, and a gorgeous guy in a white T-shirt and leather jacket struts past brick buildings, dancing a little as he waits for me to pick him up in my convertible Mercedes. It doesn't even matter that when he spins in his tux, he has a bald spot, because there's the **TANG** of that tin-can beat and I'm moving so smooth and perfect. The music is so intense it hurts, a beautiful hurt. I mouth the words along with Pebbles, but I'm talking to the floor because I *do* want to do things to a boy, just like she says, but I don't know what those things *are*.

It feels so *good*, so *good* to be here, and I want to do *everything* when the next song rolls in with the long horns blowing like the king is on his way. They hold out that last note and it's **Yeahhh** in that gravel voice, like the ogre who lives under the bridge. The drums go *tit-ta-tit-tit* as they lead into "Just Got Paid," and *every*body's feeling it. The whole club is in on it. The singer—he *knows* Club 12 feels just like the city in his video. In it, he hops out of his BMW and claps hands with the guys out front of the club. They're all wearing their Ricky Ricardo suits and doing that clap-heel-spin that makes you feel like life, life, life and everybody in it is A-okay. I feel like I'm greased when the horns and drums yell back and every person in this place *knows* how to move, and we're all one party—*say ho! Ho!*—and, fuck, do I feel *good*.

Then the "Hit-it!" and **BOOM-chicka** drums of "It Takes Two to Make a Thing Go Right" kick in. And everybody, including me, jumps up and claps because they're *psyched* about this song.

But the quickness of the **BOOM-chicka** is actually pretty

confusing. The only way to dance to it is to shake your butt and hips like a baby rattle, front and back, like the girl in the video. But that's not for me. I don't work that fast, and neither do any of the guys, because suddenly all of them, plus me, are walking off the dance floor. It's just Deanna and a couple other girls baby-rattle dancing, while hundreds of everybody else stands on the sidelines watching them. It doesn't feel like heaven anymore; it feels kind of embarrassing. Because we all *thought* we were so pumped for this song, but then we all got busted.

Then the DJ decides he can sneak in some crappy non-dance songs, now that everyone's off the floor and in a bad mood. He puts on Def Leppard's "Pour Some Sugar on Me," which is *ick*. Something about it feels like bathrooms and stepfathers. But not for Deanna. She's in *her* own little world now, dancing with her eyes closed and her arms up over her head, doing hand motions like she's climbing the rope for the Presidential Fitness Test. So for her, heaven is pantomiming the worst part of gym class. I never said we were alike, though. Just that we're best friends.

The DJ makes us like him again by putting on "Da Butt," which starts with the sound of a cheering, happy crowd. It works like subliminal advertising, because everyone is jammed back on the dance floor, and even though nobody knows exactly how to dance to this song, everybody has a butt they can circle around.

Before we know it, it's midnight and Deanna and I have to go, so I'm home by curfew. It *kills* to leave, but we get another miracle for our exit. The crowd of smokers outside the door clears when Deanna and I step out. It's like we're girl Moseses, and they're the Red Sea. Half of them move to the left, half of them move to the right, and the paved path is cleared in front of us. We strut down it as best we can in our high, high heels. I swear there should be a cameraman around, because we look just like the chicks in an Aerosmith video, tossing our hair and laughing and knowing that we're the guys' favorite. And damn. Just, damn.

23

SEPTEMBER 1989
TWO YEARS AND SIX MONTHS OUT

Remember the first time you saw *The Wizard of Oz*? Remember how shocked you were when all the color came on in Munchkinland? That's how my life feels. Everything is *good* all of a sudden. Even the bad stuff.

For example, we got new seats yesterday in social studies. I was put behind Doug Bianchi, this total popular kid, who's short but makes up for it with muscles. Doug turned around to talk to Mia Esposito, who was saying, "Ohh my God, I drank too much this weekend." And Doug went, "*You?!* I poured vodka on my Wheaties this morning!" And I didn't even wig out. I didn't laugh, of course, but I didn't wig either. Then, with me sitting right there between him and Mia, Doug kept the conversation going.

"*We* know why you get drunk on the weekend, Mia," he said. "But your secret's safe with us. Right, Cyndy?"

I just smiled and looked down at my notebook, because I *think* I get it, but then again, I don't. He's talking about sex, right? Without actually *saying* it? I don't know, but he drummed his fingers on my desk before he turned around, which means... Well, it means *some*thing.

I've actually been coming to school again. It started because of my sister's announcement, which made me *extra* not want to be in that house. Ever since she told my mother what was happening, I've had this feeling like there are ghosts—mean, tricky things I can sense, but I can't see—behind every wall. I'd rather be at school than in an empty, creepy house. And when I came back to class, I realized Masuk isn't hell anymore. With Prozac and Deanna, it's actually kind of okay. Plus, it's my senior year. If I'm gonna get into college and get out of here, I've gotta get some decent grades on my transcript.

The best part about coming back is that we're writing in Mrs. Skinner's class. Last night the homework was to go outside and write about whatever you noticed. The only rule was you had to use each of your five senses. I promised myself I wouldn't talk about stupid fall leaves, so here's what I came up with instead.

gone

the halfway point between here & there,
now & then,
is a big high rock on an old man's lawn.

it feels like scraped knees.
it looks like bad weather.

i can see from up here, like Sacajawea.
the light in the past. the dark in the future.

it sounds like the wind.
it tastes like bit tongue.

but i'm Sacajawea in reverse.
i am Aewajacas.

my past feels dark, but
my future looks light.

so i can taste freedom.
and i can smell fate.

so i'm going.
i go.

i'm gone.

It's so frigging nice out today, Mrs. Skinner goes, "Come on. We're having class outside." And we sit in a circle on the grass, a Frisbee-throw from where I decided not to kill myself. Before Skinner can say anything, someone goes, "Let's hear Cyndy's."

Swear

to

God.

"Let's hear Cyndy's."

Sometimes, someone says you don't have to pay for the donuts. Sometimes, someone says they want to hear your writing. And that niceness, that one tiny niceness, it makes up for everything else.

So I read it. My poem with "Aewajacas," which I don't even know how to say. Everyone's quiet. They listen. And they clap. They clap. "You're a writer," Jack says. So it doesn't even matter that on the way back inside, Wendi Rosini puts on her sneeze face and ignores my question about where she gets her hair done. Because I'm a *writer.* What else matters?

Being a writer is what's gonna get me outta here and into Smith College. But I shouldn't even need extra ammunition. Like I said, Smith is automatically letting me in, because it's destiny. And because I'm the daughter of their famous dead professor Alvin Etler. My mother told me Smith is so proud of him, they had this three-dimensional plaque made of his *face,* and put it front and center in their music building. So they'll jump at the chance to have his kid come to their school. I mean, they *have* to. Right?

Yeah, so...we're going. To Smith. Me and my mother. Which is weird. I have to sit in a car with her for three hours each way and talk to her about... About what? The last long car ride I had with my mother was when she tricked me into going to Straight. Maybe we can talk about *that*.

Of course, once we get to campus, my mother's gonna be all sickly sad and sensitive about *her* Alvin Etler and *her* lost innocence and, just, gag me. No, wait—do over. She'll be all *maudlin* and *treacly*. If I want to impress Smith College, I've got to start using my SAT words.

It's Saturday night and we're at Club 12. I'm having one of those *Wizard of Oz* color moments, because this boy chose *me*. Out of all the females at Club 12—including Deanna!—he chose *me*. I sit down during a slow jam, and this kid sits next to me and goes, "Hi." But he's *cute*. We kind of yell in each other's ears for a little bit—"I like your shoes" kind of stuff—before he goes, "I can't really hear you, and I *really* can't dance. Want to take a walk?"

Do I? I've been waiting my whole life.

Now we're sitting at the top of this slope, where the road curves around into the parking lot. Cars are coming into

Club 12, their headlights sliding over the slope, but the drivers don't see us, because nobody thinks to look up. We're hiding in plain sight. We're in our own little heaven.

We're talking, but not a lot.

"Yeah, shit's not so good at my place, y'know?" the cute boy says.

"Yeah," I say back.

"My old man, he wants things a certain way."

"Yeah?"

"Yeah. And I get it. I mean, it's his house, and he works all day getting his hands dirty to pay the bills, and what right do I have? I don't."

"Yeah."

"But when he comes home after the bar, he likes to pick a fight, you know?"

"Yeah," I say. Me and my SAT vocab. But he must not mind, because he just picked up my hand. Now we're in extra-heaven.

"And since my ma died, it's like he's gotten extra-picky."

"Yeah." Is this kid, like, the guy version of me?

"So that's why I come here. I want to be around people who *don't* spend their nights drinking, you know?"

"Wait—you're not program?"

"Nah. I mean, I know all about it, because my pop used to go to meetings all the time. I wish he still was. He quit, but…I don't know. I just feel good around sober people."

Fuck! He's still cute, but now he seems scary. Because he tricked me. He's not sober? But he's at a sober dance! I came out here with him, and he's not sober?!

"You're not sober?"

"Right now? Right now, I am one hundred percent sober. But in general? AA-wise? Not exactly."

"Wait, I thought—"

"Here's the deal. I don't party because I don't *want* to party. But I *can*. I can have some beers and a good time and be done with it, if I want. I'm not an *addict*, is what I'm saying. Believe it or not, there are people who can choose to have a little and then choose to stop."

This…this is crazy. He's talking in some Martian language. I don't even know what to say to this craziness. So instead, I lift my hand away from his and wrap my arms around my knees. This way, I've got my heart sheltered from this cute, dangerous, not-sober boy.

He pulls his knees up the same way I have mine, and we sit and watch the cars and trucks rip past on 95. Sometimes a car slows and gets off at exit 19, and my heart jumps a little for them.

"We should get some spray paint and graffiti the exit 19 sign," I say.

"What?" he says, laughing.

"'Welcome to Narnia,' it should say. Exit 19. Club 12. It's Narnia, you know? A magical place for desperate searchers."

"*You're* magical," he says. To me. Cyndy Etler.

He unwraps an arm from his knees, and he tilts up my chin with his fingertips. He looks at me. Smiling.

"How's *your* life?" he asks.

"Better," I say.

"Than what?"

"Than ever."

"That's cool."

"Yeah."

"I could like you," he says.

"Why?" I say back.

"*Why*? Because you just said 'why.' Because you're a good listener. Because you want to graffiti a highway sign. Because you're beautiful."

He thinks I'm someone else. Someone not me. That keeps happening, ever since I turned skinny: people think I'm some happy, simple girl. How do I learn how to be that girl?

The cute boy leans over, pressing his knees and thighs against my knees and thighs. And he kisses me. Just once. On the mouth. It's the nicest thing anyone's ever said to me.

"I guess I could like you too," I say.

He laughs. "Didn't you say you had a curfew?" He stands, then holds out a hand to help me up. "C'mon, let's find your friend and get you home."

I break Deanna's eardrums on the ride back to Monroe. "Steven. His name is Steven Ross. He's from Bridgeport. I love Bridgeport! He took my number, Dee. He's so *sweet*! Do you think he'll call me? Tomorrow? We gotta go back next weekend! Wait, am I going to Northampton next weekend? Will I be at Smith? Okay, two weeks from now. We *gotta*! Promise? Oh my *God* is he cute!"

Deanna always waits for me to get inside my house before she leaves. So the Oldsmobile is thrumming behind me as I look in the big kitchen window at the clock: 12:40. I'm ten minutes late. Crap.

I'm so excited about cute-but-not-sober Steven Ross, I can barely get my key in the lock. I finally manage to **schlunk** unlock the door, but something's wrong. The door is blocked. I can move it a couple millimeters. That's it.

Through the window, in the light from the stove, I can see the kitchen table. My mother's got her Honey Bunches of Oats waiting for her next to a spoon and a cereal bowl. She set them up ten minutes ago, at 12:30. At my curfew. She set them up, then bolted the door with the slide lock, locking me out.

I stand on the doorstep a second, thinking about boxers. I bet this is how they feel right before they fall over. This is the feeling of a knockout punch.

Deanna's messing with the radio when I reopen the passenger-side door.

"You wanna stay over tonight?" she goes.

I sob, instead of nod.

"Come on. My mom found fucking Sweet'N Low ice cream!"

She wheels the Oldsmobile and floors it down the drive-way. Her tires throw rocks back at the big front kitchen window.

24

My mother and I, we're good at pretending shit never happened. We go the whole ride to Northampton with nobody bringing up her locking me out of the house. Instead, she spends the trip talking about her diet, her aerobics teaching, and how Smith will definitely want me because I'm a "legacy." Which doesn't mean I'm a famous person who's done important things; it means I'm the kid of someone who graduated from Smith. Namely, her.

Smith is okay looking, I guess. Lots of brick and ivy with a swirly, black metal gate out front, as if Count Dracula lives there. It's the campus version of that lady who goes, "Oh, this old rag?" when you compliment her dress.

First thing after we park, we go to Sage Hall, which is Smith's music building. We walk in the front door, and there it is: the side view of my father's head and shoulders, made out of bronze. My mother says it's not a plaque, it's a "bust." Which sounds pretty embarrassing, if you ask me.

My mother keeps herself in check. She doesn't make a big scene about how she's Alvin Etler's widow. Maybe it's because we're running late for my interview, which is held upstairs in the admissions building, in one of those chilly rooms with dark-green carpet and windows that seem like they've never been opened. It smells like books and the 1950s.

Sitting across from my interviewer, a lady with a little gray bun, I use Straight's number one rule as my crutch: honesty. I explain how I'm a druggie and always will be, but thanks to my mother and God and Straight, Inc., I'm almost four years sober. I tell her my grades aren't that great because I was wicked depressed, but I'm doing much better now. I tell her my father taught here, and my mother went here, and I really, really want to be a writer. She doesn't necessarily smile, but I think I did okay. She gives me one piece of advice: do well on the SATs.

Afterward, my mother drives me around campus and tells me about her time at Smith. It's pretty amazing because I've never heard her talk about my father without being all weepy. She goes by this cute house and tells me she got to live there when she was a junior and a senior. She said the apartment had a kitchen and a door to outside and everything.

"How old were you then?" I go.

"Oh, it was my senior year when I met your father, so I would've been…twenty and twenty-one years old."

"You hooked up with him when you were twenty?"

"'Hooked up'? I don't know what that means. We met at the start of my senior year. I took his Advanced Theory of Music class and fell in love with his teaching. I asked him to be my thesis advisor, and I fell in love with *him*. He was… brilliant. You can't imagine. He was funny and attentive and witty, and…*everybody* loved him. His classes were the first to fill up. Standing room only. And he chose *me*."

"So you were *how* old when you guys got together? Eighteen?"

"I was a twenty-one-year-old graduating senior, and I was very much in love."

"So you were twenty-one, and he was…seventy?" I'm trying not to think my father was kind of grody. I'm trying not to think my mother was kind of desperate.

"Cynthia Drew Etler. We can stop this discussion right now."

"Sorry. It just seems kind of… I'm sorry. But how old was he when you guys got married?"

"He was an esteemed professor and composer, beloved by the Smith community."

"And he was born in like 1910, so he would've been…"

"He was *not* born in 1910. He was fifty-three years old when we married, but the age difference didn't matter a bit, because we were so in love. Nothing else matters when two people are in love."

I guess I see her point, maybe. But still. He was fifty-three. She was twenty-one. That would be like me marrying a forty-nine-year-old. And *ewww*.

The conversation comes to a halt when my mother parks the car by these little stores. She *never* takes me shopping, unless it's for mark-down groceries or thrift-store school clothes. But today we're going in some overpriced trinket shops?

"Your father would come here to buy me cards and little gifts," my mother says. She's smiling like she's talking to his ghost.

"He really loved you," I say.

"He really did," she says back.

Those are the nicest words we've said to each other in my life.

Inside the store, she goes her way and I go mine. And good thing, because I find the *perfect* gift: a little red cardboard box in the shape of a heart, with these pink and white candies that are filled with chocolate. I have to use half my monthly food allowance, but it's worth it, 'cause like my mother said: when you're in love, nothing else matters.

"Do you want a box for this?" the cashier asks, tilting my heart to study how cute it is.

"Yes!" I say back. "That's perfect! Then I can wrap it and send it through the mail."

"Someone will be happy when they open it. Who's the lucky someone?"

"A boy," I say, and look back to make sure my mother's not eavesdropping. "A boy named Steven Ross."

25

OCTOBER 1989
TWO YEARS AND SEVEN MONTHS OUT

I am the last person to have not had sex. I'm the Last Virgin Standing.

I tried to meet Jack and Whitney on Saturday night, right? Friday was sub day in band again, and Jack yelled to everyone, "*Rocky Horror*! Saturday midnight! Milford Cinema! Be there!" On Saturday, Deanna mysteriously "couldn't come out," and my mother mysteriously let me take the car, so I went to Milford Cinema. I got my ticket and stood there on the sidewalk like a super-ultra-megaloser, but nobody from school showed up. Still, I had already paid. So at 11:59 I slunk into the farthest back row and had the seams of my life ripped open.

The Rocky Horror Picture Show is the other half of the rainbow. It's the dark version of all the colors. Remember that Crayola art project where you covered every inch of a piece of paper with all the best crayons in swirling swoops, then you colored over the whole page in black? It looked all dark and icky until you scratched a nail through the black, and **schzing!** Color! *Rocky Horror* is like that art project. It teaches you that what looks bleak and dark is actually bright and beautiful; you just can't see it until you scratch the surface.

Monday when I see Jack, I can't stop myself. I'm all, "OhmyGod, *The Rocky Horror Picture Show*? It's all about *sex!*"

Jack smiles like the bald butler and goes, "Isn't everything?"

And Whitney blushes. She *blushes*. Which means they *do* it.

I am the *last* person to have not had sex.

Maybe I wouldn't be so last if Steven Ross had called me. Which he didn't. I looked in the phone book and found one Steven Ross—BRIDGEPORT—and sent the heart-shaped box to that address, with a note that just said, "I ❤'d Saturday night." And my phone number again, in case he lost it. And my address, in case he wanted to write back. Or visit.

It's been a month. I've been back to Club 12 on two separate Saturdays. No Steven Ross.

Maybe if I weren't such a virgin, he would've kept liking me back. I don't know. I only know that Dammit Janet was the only virgin in *The Rocky Horror Picture Show*, and she was stupid. And everybody else was cool. Which sounds about right.

———————

The mystery is solved. It's not that Deanna couldn't go out Saturday night; it's that she couldn't go out with *me*. She had to go out with her *boy*friend.

She introduces me to him by bringing him to my house. Swear to God. I see her car rolling up the driveway, and I get all excited and run downstairs. But when I get outside, it's not Deanna driving, it's this *weasel*. Seriously. The kid's whole face is long bones and a pointy nose. He looks like he just finished licking the mud off his face. He's still blinking from the shock of sunlight.

Deanna jumps out of the passenger side all giggly and quick. Weasel rolls out from behind the wheel and fakes a stretch to close the door.

I look at him, he looks at me, and instantly, we don't like each other. The vibe is Wild West shootout as I stand on the front stoop, hands on hips, and he fakes another stretch, arms all wide-spread to the sides. He's gotta make himself look big, because he's not. He's a slip of a thing.

"Hey, Cyndy! This is my boyfriend, Gregory," Deanna chirps.

Greg-or-y. He makes you use three syllables. I keep my hands on my hips and my feet on the stoop. He leans to the right until his hip is on the car door.

"Come on!" Deanna says, grabbing my hands and pulling me off the stoop. "Come *meet* him!"

I raise an eyebrow at her, and she leans in to whisper in my ear. The smell of her Aussie hairspray makes me need to cry. I haven't smelled Aussie in weeks. "C'mon," she goes. "I really want you to like him."

"I'll try," I say back. "But will he like me?"

She pretends not to hear that.

"Hi, Greg," I go, not putting out a hand. "I'm Cyndy."

"So I've heard," he says, jangling Dee's keys.

I hate him. But I'll try.

———

Deanna is having sex. With a crooked penis. I shit you not.

She comes back from the dead for my birthday, which is really cool of her. I'm at my locker—basically seeing if I can fit *in* my locker, so I won't have to spend the day not hearing "happy birthday" from anyone—when I hear, "Welll...*hey!*" Which is our thing.

The first time we said it, we laughed till we peed ourselves. It was in the bathroom by the cafeteria. She wanted to smoke, and I didn't want to show my face in the smoking pit, so we compromised with the girls' lav. We were leaning on the sinks and she'd just lit her cig when the chemistry teacher cracked open the door and put her big face through.

"Welll...*hey!*" Deanna had said, zipping her cig behind her while I turned the faucet on over it.

The chem teacher shook her head and went away, while

me and Deanna laughed and laughed. And now that's our thing. "Welll...*hey!*"

"Hiii!" I say back. "What're you doing at school? I thought you were going for a world record in absences!"

"What, I'm gonna miss my best friend's eighteenth birthday? Come on!" She throws me the keys to the Oldsmobile, and I actually catch them.

"What...*skip*?! I can't! I'll get reported!"

"No you won't. Because look."

She pulls out a scrawly script note with a red-ink stamp at the bottom: APPROVED. I read the script and it says this:

To Whom It May Concern,
Please excuse Cyndy Etler from school today October
17, 1989. She has doctor and dentist appointments.

Then there's a scribble that might or might not be somebody's signature, but it worked. Deanna got me excused from school. Holy fuck.

"Welll...*hey!*" I say, with my skull hinging open and rainbows bouncing out.

"Welll...*hey!*" she says, linking her arm through mine and steering me out a side door.

We spend the day having her whole house to ourselves. Her dad's at work, and her mom's out of town. So we can talk about anything, which we do. Including Gregory's bent penis.

"You are *not*, Dee."

"I am *too*, Cynd."

"But…what's it *like*, sex? Is this your first…?"

"No, but almost. I halfway did it with a guy before I went to rehab, which is why I got sent away. My dad found my stash of rubbers."

"Ewww! Rubbers?!"

"I know, but shut up. Do *you* want to get preggers?"

"Well, first of all, I probably won't because I'm nowhere near *ever* having *sex*. And second of all, I'm on the *pill*."

"Oh yeah, that's right. God, I *wish*. My dad's like special-ordering me a chastity belt."

"But seriously—what's it like?"

"I don't know. How do you describe it? It's…sweaty. But not necessarily *your* sweat. I mean, the guy's on top of you, and he's, like, doing the heave ho, and his neck sweat falls on your face."

"Oh my *God*. Why would you even?"

"Because what comes *before* sex is *awesome*. Then you have to, like, pay him back, by letting him put it in you."

"Are you *serious*?"

"Yup. That's just the way it goes."

"So, wait. You have to tell me the whole, exact process of what happens. From the beginning. I totally can't picture how you end up getting heave-hoed."

"Okay, well, you start with kissing, obviously. And

eventually—or quickly, I guess; it depends on the guy—he puts his hands on your boobs, which feels fucking great if he knows what he's doing. You know how you rub your thumb on the top of your eraser, to get the pencil smudges off and start fresh? If he does that to your nips, *especially* over your bra, he knows what the fuck he's doing. I've even had a guy put his *mouth* on my nip over my bra, and then he like, clamped his front teeth around it a little? That almost sent me through the roof of the car."

"*Really?!* Why?"

"I dunno. It's… I dunno. It's fucking hot."

God, am I out of my league. If Dee and I did have a *Seventeen* magazine spread, the title would be *The Prom Queen and the Preschooler.* I need to catch up, quick. "Okay, so…keep going."

"So he'll undo your bra and touch your boobs for a while, and then you'll make out some more, and then he's gonna move downstairs. He's gonna try to be slick and distract you by kissing harder or kissing your neck or ear or something. Which can get really gross, really quick. But you're gonna probably pretend you don't notice his hand, because it feels great, but who wants to admit they're a slut? So you're gonna pretend you don't know what he's doing as he's moving a hand toward your undies. And then, you better look out."

"Shit. Why?"

"Because that's the point of no return."

"Waddaya mean?"

"Well, there's a lot that happens all of a sudden. One, it feels *so, fucking, good*, you don't want to tell him to stop. But if you *don't* tell him to stop, he's gonna go from hand to dick, and next thing you know, you're a pregger risk."

"Holy fuck. It just…*happens* like that? That quick?"

"Preeetty much. And the other thing is, once he gets to third base? Once he's got his finger wet and you're all *ooh-aah*? He feels like you *have* to let him get his dick wet. He made you feel good. Now you have to let *him*."

"No way."

"Yes way."

"So what happens if he gets… What happens if he gets to third base and *then* you say no? *Can* you, even?"

"Yeah, you can. But I wouldn't recommend it."

"Why not?"

"Because then you're a prick tease."

"So wait. Either you do something you don't want to do, or you get called a nasty name?"

"Huh?"

"Never mind. Just, what happens if you do it anyway? What happens if you get to third and *then* you say stop?"

"Well, hopefully he stops. And then, expect to get iced."

"Iced?"

"Yeah. Iced out. Like, no more Mr. Nice Guy. Like you're gonna be walking home. Like you're going to prom alone. You don't want to let a guy go that far and *then* cut him off. If you want to stay a virgin, keep it above the waist. Or plan to get good at BJs."

"*Blow* jobs?! Deanna!"

"I am serious. That's your only other option."

"Do *you*?!"

"Yeah, I have. It's not that bad if you know a few tricks. And if he's friendly with a bar of soap."

"Ewww! You mean it stinks?"

"Of *course* it stinks if he didn't just wash it! Think about all that jangly hot meat, crunched up and wrapped tight in undies and jeans. They walk around all day with that pile of stuff getting sweatier and sweatier with no vent, no windows. What's it supposed to smell like, fucking peach cobbler?"

"Oh. My. *God*, Deanna. I am *never*—"

"Yeah, you are. You are. 'Cause once he gets his hand down there, something changes."

"What?" I really don't know if I want to know or not. But… Yeah. I do. "What changes?"

"*You* change. It's like the switch to superhero when an emergency happens. Dude goes from mild and polite to 'Yee haw, I'll kick your ass, now watch me fly.' You make the same personality switch when a guy gets you going. But you don't turn into a superhero—you turn into an animal. You stop giving a fuck. You're like, 'Let's go.' *He* knows that, which is why he's trying to sneak his hand down there. It's up to *you* to decide, while you're still human, if you want to let yourself make that flip to *fuck it*."

"Holy shit. I don't know about all this."

"You don't have to know. It's just what happens. It's, like, natural. Didn't you learn this shit in biology class?"

"Not like *this* I didn't!"

"You know what they never taught me in bio? That dicks can get all bent up."

"Shut *up*."

"No, seriously. Gregory's dick—it's crooked."

"Whaaat?"

"For serious. It's like"—she puts her fist in the air with her arm straight out, then bends it at the elbow—"this is his dick. Swear to God! Like *this*." She shakes her bent arm a little, to make sure I notice it.

"So…what? Why?"

"He was in a scuba accident. He went too deep and lost his oxygen connection. He *raced* the fuck back to the surface, but coming up from that deep so fast, the change in pressure somehow…bent his dick."

"Is it weird?"

"The dick?"

"Yeah! Does it look weird?"

"I don't know. I mean, how many dicks do you think I've seen? I'm not the dick expert!"

"Deanna?"

"Yeah?"

"I'm moving to a convent."

26

Perry O'Sullivan is a kid who graduated last year.

Perry O'Sullivan is really cute and rich.

Perry O'Sullivan is Gregory's best friend.

Perry O'Sullivan told Gregory he thinks *I'm* cute.

Perry O'Sullivan, Gregory, Deanna, and I went on a double date.

Perry O'Sullivan asked me out again.

Perry O'Sullivan took me to his house when his parents weren't home.

Perry O'Sullivan is really cute. And rich.

Perry O'Sullivan started kissing me.

Perry O'Sullivan wanted to take a shower with me.

Perry O'Sullivan laughed when I said I was too nervous.

Perry O'Sullivan said wearing his boxers over my undies in the shower was really stupid.

Perry O'Sullivan got mad when I stepped into, then right out of the shower.

Perry O'Sullivan doesn't know my little sister said her father made her shower with him.

Perry O'Sullivan stayed in the shower when I left his house.

Perry O'Sullivan hasn't called me since that day.

…and neither has Deanna.

Deanna finally called to tell me she has a new boyfriend. Only he's a *man*. He lives in New York City; he's some kind of plumber; he owns a business. Deanna has a *man*friend.

She's been taking her car into the city and staying with him. In his apartment. Above his plumbing store. I swear to God. She tells her dad she's staying at my house, and she just...*goes*. I know she only called to make sure I'll stay her alibi. After three months with zero friends, though, I don't even care.

Why *should* I care what her reasons are, because we're *here*! In the city! Right *now*! It's un-be-fucking-lievable! When we got here, Deanna drove around the block for forty-five minutes, looking for a parking space. Finally, she goes, "Fuck this," and slams on the brakes, double-parking next to a spot that's "reserved." She stalks over to the traffic cone and folding chair in the should've-been-empty spot, and she, like, *throws* them up on the sidewalk. Then she's back in the car doing this bullet-smooth parallel park, talking the whole time, like, "Fuck-kin, shove yer cone up your *ass*. Not *your* patch of pavement. Key my car. Watch what happens. My boyfriend sells metal *pipe* for a living."

"Dee?"

"What."

"Who're you talking to?"

"Cunts. Come on."

She grabs her fringed black leather purse and her Marlboro Lights and slams her door, hard. But once we get walking, she calms down.

"So here's the deal. Glen's taking us out to eat"—Glen is Deanna's manfriend—"and later, we're meeting up with Curtis." Curtis is *Glen's* best friend, and also, Curtis is a *male model*. "There's no extra room at Glen's place, so you can stay at Curtis's."

"Um, Dee?"

"Yeah."

"How old is Curtis again?"

"Same as Glen. Like twenty-eight, twenty-nine."

"And he's…does he know I'm a virgin?"

"He's *not* gonna try to rape you, Cyndy. Promise."

"Or shower with me?"

"Here! Look! Glen's store!"

It's a beautiful store. Picture the main stoop on Sesame Street, where everyone meets. On the right side is Oscar the Grouch's garbage can, but have you ever noticed on the left side is a little gate with a ground-floor window behind it? That's where Glen's store is: below street level, behind a window, with stairs leading *down* to it from the sidewalk. It's *so* cool.

As we go down the stairs, I have to make myself not do something corny, like grab Deanna's hand and kiss it. Because how is this even happening to me? It's Friday night and I'm in the city with no grown-up, no staff, going underground into a store to hang with the *owner*. Like, no *way*.

Glen's really different from Gregory. He weighs more than a hundred pounds, for one thing, and his face is red, not gray. But Glen's not the main attraction; his store is. It's like a dollhouse blown up to human size, with perfect mini-bathrooms everywhere you look. There's one for every kind of millionaire, manly-man to girly-girl. You can tell who each one is for by the color of the wood in the cabinets and how much decoration is on the knobs and faucets. There's even, way in the back, a plain old small-tub bathroom for regular people. But the prize—the pièce de résistance—is the golden tub on a pedestal right in front of the window. I barely say hi to Glen before beelining over and petting it.

"You're right, Dee Dee. She *is* a hippie," Glen says. He comes over to the tub and turns on the faucet.

"It works!" I say. Okay, I squeal. "You could take a bath *right here*, next to this giant window, with all of Manhattan walking past?"

"All of Brooklyn, but yeah." He's smiling. Guys always look cuter when they smile. "And here, check this out." He points at some silver buttons next to the faucet. "When the tub fills up, these make the magic."

"What magic?!"

"Bubbles. And colored lights."

"Who can afford this? How much would this cost?"

"More than a new Toyota but less than a new Porsche. You wanna get in?"

"What, *now*?" I say, looking around. There's nobody in here but us, but still.

"Sure, why not? I close in twenty minutes, and it takes that long for this thing to fill. I'll lock the door and turn off the lights, and you can have at it. That way Dee Dee and I can go upstairs and get reacquainted."

Deanna giggles. Gag me. But I squealed. So gag her too.

When Glen clicks off the lights, he goes out the door first. Before Deanna follows him, she looks back at me with a smile so big her eyes crinkle.

"Welll...*hey!*" she whispers.

"Welll...*hey!*" I whisper back. Right now, I'd rate my life a ten.

It's not even nerve-wracking, taking off my clothes in

view of a giant window, because to see me, someone would have to bend themself in half and get their eyes down to foot level. I know because all I can see through the window are the heels and ankles of the people walking past.

I slide into the purple-pink-blue hot bubbling water. I'm literally locked in here, safe and alone, watching as the whole world clicks and stomps past. I see them, but they can't see me. I'll stay here forever, please.

———

Glen takes us on the subway to some Chinese food place, the kind where the only menu is the huge plastic one hung over the counter, with the blown-up photos of General Tso's and egg foo young. I have chicken and broccoli, no rice, but God. Why is food so good in New York? How do New Yorkers stay so skinny when even lame Chinese is the best thing you've ever eaten? Glen talks the whole time we're eating. "Now you're in Manhattan," he says, shooting a grain of rice out of his mouth at me. I don't want to embarrass him, so I leave it sitting there on my boob. "Look out the window. See the diff?" I don't, but I'm not telling him that.

Curtis meets us on the street, and we all start walking. Actually, we all stand still while Curtis looks me up and down and nods and says, "hey," then turns and starts walking with Glen. Deanna follows them, and I follow Deanna.

Curtis is okay-looking. I guess I expected more from a

male model, but whatever. I don't need to look at some guy when there's so much else to see. Like the angled wooden crates of fruit, bright red and yellow, arranged in perfect, shining rows, out front of the tiny grocery stores. And the hundreds of bundles of flowers, stacked up like buckets of hope. Like someone's gonna buy all these flowers before they die? But someone does. Guys and girls, still in their work clothes, are buzzing over them like bees. Like they want a piece of nature in the middle of all this concrete.

And the faces—the faces! The straight-ahead stares, and the tight-rolled newspapers tucked into armpits, and that New York stride. And the black sheets spread out, right on the sidewalk, with purses and jewelry and old magazines wrapped in plastic. The Jamaican guy with the fanny pack talks to me, to Deanna, to the businesswomen: "Hey, pretty lady, you know you need some sparkle for them ears! Hooold up!"

Everyone but me pretends to not hear him, but I smile and say, "No thanks." I love him, I think, for putting old magazines in plastic, for that hope that somebody will buy them.

I'm so caught up in everything, like a kid at fucking Disney World, I almost step on him. The man on the sidewalk. I hope this doesn't make me stupid, but I stop. I can't move. Because he's *sleeping* here. How can he fall asleep with thousands of people walking by his face? Where *is* he, in his mind, that he can fall asleep on a January night on a sidewalk in New York City? Where are *we,* that we can walk right past him? I can't. Literally. I don't know or care where Deanna is; I can't walk past this man.

He's huddled against the wall of one of the tiny grocery stores. So I go in and unfold my one soft five-dollar bill, and I tell the man behind the counter, "There's a bum sleeping outside your store. Can I buy him this banana? And these bagel chips?"

The man doesn't answer me, he just waves his hand over the food like a magician. Or like, *Get out of here.*

I can't say I'm not nervous, putting the banana and the bagel chips by the man. I'm *wicked* nervous. If he wakes up and some stranger's right next to him, he'll freak. So I feel pretty shitty about it, but I put the stuff on the ground and kind of push it toward his face with my foot. I tell him, "I hope this is okay with you. I hope you don't mind. I thought you were probably hungry."

"CYNDY!" If Deanna's screech didn't wake him up, maybe he's more than just sleeping. "What are you—*get!* Come *on!*"

"Dee, I couldn't *leave* him there!"

"Well, I almost left *you*, stupid! Let's go."

She grabs my hand and drags me up the street and away from the man. When I look back, I can still see the red-and-white bagel chip bag, untouched. Then we turn the corner.

———

"You guys have to go first," Curtis says, pushing me and Deanna in front of him and Glen. "Don't smile. And stick your tits out. We'll be back here. It just can't look like you have guys with you. Now *go*." He pushes a finger in my spine like it's a gun.

I glance at Deanna, but she doesn't look back at me. She shakes her head and says, "Aerosmith video."

And I get it. It works. I'm a different person; I'm that girl with the open lips, the hair flounce, the strut. Deanna is too. We tits-out-no-smile step right past all the hair-sprayed, purple-makeupped, black-outfitted people in line trying to get into the club. We Aerosmith-chick right up to the guy guarding the door.

"Ay! Ayyy!" we hear from the pissed off line of suckers behind us. But Aerosmith girls don't give a fuck. We just shake out our hair and reset our shoulders.

"Yeah, we're on the list," Deanna says, looking at the guy and snapping her gum.

"Oh yeah?" he says. His upper arms are the size of honey hams. They pop around as he lifts up his clipboard.

"Ohhh yeah," Deanna says. She puts her arm around my middle, pushing our hips toward him. "Me and my girl-friend. We're riiggghhht...*there*." She points a red talon at a spot on his clipboard.

The guy looks from his clipboard to her lips to my boobs. I force myself to not cave them inward.

194

"C'mon," he says, unhooking the velvet rope. "The two a ya."

It's Deanna who squeals this time. "Thank you!" She goes up on tiptoe and kisses him on the cheek, then leans past his bulldozer belly to tell Curtis and Glen, "We're in!"

We fly past the door guy and into the club before he can change his mind, and then Curtis and Glen are behind us, slapping each other five. "We biffed the line at the Roxy, man!" Curtis says. Or rather, he yells. It's frigging loud in here.

It's a good thing I got to practice being a video girl outside, because when we push open the doors from the black-lit hallway into the actual club, we *are* in a video. Swear to God. The disco ball is spinning, and the spotlight is swooping, and the electrocuted **skdd-dit!dit!dit!** of "I've Got the Power" clicks on, like it had been waiting for us.

The woman yells the refrain, and the drum comes up from under my feet with a round sound, as if it's getting hit inside a big metal bowl. The cowbells are circular too—they end on the up, like a question mark—and I'm possessed. I'm drugged by the voodoo of the music. I don't know, don't care, forget about Deanna as I float into the edges and get swallowed by the crowd.

The singer's kind of moaning now, and all of us soar and swim on her words, then pound like jackbooted Germans when the **skdd-dit!dit!dit!** comes back. Nothing matters—not how we look or who we're with or what our

little sister told our mother about Jacque. It doesn't matter.
It's all gone. We're in this trance, this music, this other perfect place.

And then the air is cracked in half by "Everybody dance,
now!" and everybody does. We're not at Club 12. We're in
Manhattan, where people *know* how to fucking dance. I'm
kicked in the shin by a black guy doing the Running Man,
and when I turn to watch him, there's Deanna, right next
to me, moving her arms in shapes up over her head, like an
updated version of the YMCA.

I grab her and pull her back as three guys in baggy pant-
suits do midair splits when the song says to jump. These
dudes are tearing. It. *Up.* The spotlight spins over to them
as we all clear a circle to kind of keep dancing, but mostly
to watch these fucking masters at work. We're trying not to
stroke out from happiness, because *we are* the party people in
the house, and who knew it could feel this *good*?

Then, from every speaker, we hear this Martian's voice
telling us, "*Jam!*" The beat kicks in like rubber balls, like
drumsticks on upside-down plastic buckets. My heart shat-
ters in a million tiny valentines because this song, this club,
it feels like frigging nirvana, like we're dancing on frigging
Sesame Street. Everyone's black and white and brown and
happy, and everyone's like, "Damn, you look *good*!"

The baggy-pants dancers are still doing their thing, and if
this is what heaven feels like, I want to die right now. The

song is carnival piano, the Martian telling us "J-*jam!*" and the horns going dum-dum-didee, making sure that we all do.

Until Curtis and Glen put a stop to this nonsense.

"Let's go," I hear, kidnapper-close to my ear.

Suddenly we're back in the black-lit hallway, heading the wrong direction, and Glen's saying something about "colored people music." I can't decide if I want to punch him or cry or suicide dive back into the dancing crowd. Man. Deanna has *really* bad taste in boyfriends.

Curtis didn't eat dinner, so we leave heaven to go to a greasy spoon. All I'm allowed is black coffee with Sweet'N Low, so that's what I'm having. The guys have brown-edged grilled cheese and Deanna is eating Glen's fries.

"How the fuck did you *do* that?" Glen asks. He looks at Deanna, then me.

"Easy," Dee says. "We just pretended we were doing an Aerosmith video."

Glen spits out his Coke laughing, and Curtis goes, "Yeah!" so hard it almost sounds like "*Jam!*" Then Curtis leans over and high-fives me, like I'm part of the win.

"Oh, you guys like Aerosmith?" I ask, because this is my great opportunity. I have something unbelievable to share, something nobody else has. "So, listen: Steven Tyler, right?"

"Duh," Glen says, but I can tell he's a little bit interested.

"He spoke at my rehab." The diner goes silent, as if even the cook wants to hear my story. "Seriously! This was after they moved me from the Virginia Straight to the Boston Straight. They wanted us to get comfortable with AA, so they started holding AA meetings Saturday nights at the building. Even non-Straightlings could come. Of course, only third-, fourth-, and fifth-phasers could go, because what, they're gonna carry newcomers in by the belt loop in front of outsiders? *Not!*"

Not a single fork is clinking; not a single coffee cup is rattling. It's like that time I told group how my mother's husband beat me: every single person is interested. In *me*.

"So this one fifth-phaser had been going to Boston meetings, right? And so was Steven Tyler. Dude *met* Steven Tyler. At an AA meeting. And asked him if he'd come speak. So fucking Steven Tyler, of Aerosmith, comes in to Straight Boston and tells his story. To all the third-, fourth-, and fifth-phasers, and all the AA outsiders and everybody. Except me."

A knife clang-a-clang-a-clangs to the floor.

"That was the weekend, after fourteen months in the building, that they let me go back to my mother's house in Connecticut. I was there, flipping out about my druggie fucking high school, while Steven fucking Tyler was speaking to the Boston Straightlings."

"Fourteen months?" Curtis says.

"Well, sixteen months, actually. But it took me fourteen

to get to fifth phase. And you can't go home until you're on fifth, if you're an out-of-towner."

"Huh?" Curtis says.

"How old were you?" Glen asks.

"When Steven Tyler spoke? Fifteen," I say.

"And you'd already been in rehab for fourteen months?" Glen asks.

"Yeah," I say.

There's a long silence, like after someone farts in the bathroom stall at school.

"*God*," Curtis says finally. "What were you, shooting smack in the bassinet?"

Glen and Curtis laugh at that, and the diner comes back to life. Deanna's digging through her bag, not looking at me, and I'm sitting here feeling extra-stupid. Not only did I say something weird and wrong, but I don't even know what it *was*. I guess I shouldn't talk about Straight to outsiders? This is what I get for breaking Straight's most important rule: What you see here, what you hear here, what you do here remains here.

After the diner, out on the sidewalk, Curtis goes, "Let's take a walk."

"Where?" Deanna asks. "I mean, I've got these heels on…"

"Suck it up, crybaby," he says back. "We're going to Central Park."

"*Now?!*" That's me. "Isn't it midnight?"

Nobody answers because some dude's getting out of a cab at the curb and Glen's yelling, "Ours! Taxi!"

We all smash in the back, and Deanna and me are *rolling* 'cause the taxi driver's hauling *ass* like **bee-beeeeeeep** and running red lights, and we're probably gonna die, but we'll die laughing. The guys are paying for everything and really, when you think about it, Central Park at midnight sounds pretty fucking cool.

When we get out of the cab, I want to stop and talk to the horses standing around with their carriages. But I can tell it's not time for that. Deanna and Glen are already up ahead, walking in a snuggle like a Judy Blume dream couple. And Curtis is putting his arm around me like he wants to snuggle-walk too.

"Are they nice to the horses?" I ask him.

"Of course. Otherwise, the horses would quit working for them."

"No, I'm serious. It's got to hurt, walking around on pavement all day. Do they get to be someplace grassy sometimes?"

"They do. I promise. The city has rules the drivers have to follow. The horses get a certain number of hours on soft ground a day."

This might be stupid, but when he says that, I get tears in my eyes. Maybe because I'm so happy for the horses. Or maybe because I'm so happy he took my question seriously.

If we keep talking about the horses I'll start bawling, so I go, "Where's Deanna?"

"Up ahead. We're going to meet them at the pond. Trust me," he says. And we walk.

I don't know why everyone acts like Central Park is the boogeyman's turf, because we see nobody, not even a bum on a park bench. Nobody, only trees and bushes and rocks and the winding, paved path. All I have to do is ask Curtis one question—"You're really a model?"—and he talks and talks about department stores and shoots and portfolios and angles and lighting. Then, right before I can say, "Wait, you put on makeup?" we're at this little lake. Deanna and Glen are already there, unsmooshing from each other.

"Cyndy!" Glen yells. "You want to go out?" He thumbs at a bunch of rowboats stacked against a hut.

I look at Deanna. She goes, "Welll…" and I go "…*hey!*"

And we're laughing and laughing because where the fuck *are* we and whose life *is* this, and we're gonna get rowed around a little lake by suitors, like some painting from 1910.

The guys are laughing too. They're heaving a rowboat off the stack and twisting oars out of the bundle and coffin-carrying the boat to the edge of the water.

"Get in!" Glen says.

Deanna steps into the pointy end, high heels and all. The boat's rocking around a little, since Glen pushed it into the water, so Curtis holds my hand to help me in. I'm getting my butt balanced on the middle bench when the boat makes this rocky-scrapey sound. It's moving. Out into the water.

I twist around and the guys are behind me, at the back, bending their arms to do a big final push. "Come on, get in!" I say. "You're gonna get your pants wet!"

They're laughing like Dee and I were a minute ago, their faces squinched with the effort of the shove. The oars are still over by the hut.

"Come on!" I semi-scream as the boat slips forward.

"Oars!" Deanna yells as the rowboat keeps moving. I turn forward—we're almost at the middle of the pond—and whip back to see the guys run off into the dark of the trees. Fucking, *fuck*.

Now I know how New Yorkers stay so slim with all this killer food everywhere. They live whole lifetimes in a single frigging night. It's 3:00 a.m., and tonight I rode two hours into the city, hunted down a parking space, took a bath in a golden tub, ate killer Chinese, jumped the line at a club, danced with fucking pros, humiliated myself at a diner, paraded through Central Park, and got stranded in a lake with my best-best friend. In ten New York hours, I had more fun than in all the combined hours of the past eighteen years.

Deanna and Glen took a taxi back to Glen's place, and Curtis and I took a taxi back to his. I tried to tell Dee we should just head home, but Glen yanked her into a hug before I could get a word out.

So now I'm at Curtis's place, and I'm pretty tired. I'd like to sleep. Curtis is pretty awake. He'd like to not sleep.

As soon as we get in his apartment, he starts kissing me. Which is kind of okay. I mean, male model, right? But then he's trying to do more, which is kind of not okay. After a minute he starts moving his hands from my middle toward my bra. I'm like, *Whoa, Nelly*, so I catch his hands with mine and lean back away from him, like we're square dancing. He's game enough—he keeps his feet toe-to-toe with mine, so I can swing back and forth on our arms— but I can tell by his expression he won't play this game for long.

"Let me ask you a question," I say.

"Only if I can ask you a question," he says.

"You first," I say.

"How long have you been out of rehab?" he asks.

"Two years and ten months," I say, swinging faster.

"So you're eighteen?"

"Yeah. How old are you?"

"Is that your question?"

"What?"

"You said you had a question."

"Oh! No, my *real* question is, why'd you guys push us out in the rowboat?"

He lets go of my hands so fast I fall back on his bed, and he's clapping. And laughing. "Was that not the funniest shit you've *ever*?! You should've seen you two, trying to paddle with your *hands!*"

"I mean, yeah, it was pretty funny. Someday I'll definitely die laughing, telling my grandkids about being stranded in a rowboat in the Central Park pond, at one a.m. in January. And I'll really roll when I tell them about getting whacked in the shoulder by a flying oar, and paddling to get to where the other oar landed in the water."

He sits on the bed next to me. Too close.

"Yeah, I'm sorry about that," he says. "Let me kiss it and make it better." He's pulls my shirt off my shoulder and leans his head in.

"No, no, I'm fine." I try to pull my shirt back up, but he won't let me. He's pulling it in the other direction. Half of my bra is uncovered.

"No, I'm *fine! Really!*" I lean away from him, and he's on me hard and quick, like a lion who's been *waiting* for this zebra.

"No!" I push him off easy with the weird Hulk strength I would get, before Straight, when I fought my step-siblings. I'm up from the bed with my shirt half-off and my jacket half-on. I'm opening all six locks on his door and spitting out gibberish, like, "Get me the fuck outta here, get me the *fuck*…" I get the last lock open and I'm hard-clacking down all the flights of marble stairs, and thank God, thank *God*, there's a taxi. I put my arm out and it comes to me, like witchcraft.

Then I'm in the backseat saying, "I don't know where it is," to the nice brown eyes looking back at me in the rearview. "I just know the name."

"Okay," the driver says. His accent makes the letters crisp as toast. "You tell me name. I get you there."

"It's a store," I say. "Brooklyn Tile and Bath."

"Brook-lin Tile and Bat," he says back, then leans over his passenger seat and pulls something out from underneath it. A yellow pages. He starts flipping through the book and tracing his finger down the page, like this is just what superheroes do. I can hear him whispering, "Brook-lin Tile. Brook-lin Tile."

Then he sits up, shifts into drive—**chunk-chunk**—and pulls the cab into the street. I lean back and exhale a bagpipe's worth of air. I didn't even notice I wasn't breathing.

There's a little flag hanging from his rearview. It has a crescent moon and star on it. The flag and me are swaying back and forth, in sync, as he quietly drives along the almost-empty streets.

"I like your flag," I say. "It's pretty."

He looks at me in the rearview. I can tell by the crinkle of his eyes that he's smiling.

We ride along, me and the flag rocking gently, when my brain wakes up. "Fuck! Wait!" I say. "Fuck! I'm so sorry, but I—I'm sorry!" I'm trying really hard not to cry. I'm failing. "I have no money! I spent my last money! I'm so—"

"It's ok," he says, his words toast-crisp. "I give you a ride."

When he pulls over, there's the big belowground window. In the soft yellow store lights, I can see the base of the golden bathtub. I was in that tub so long ago, it feels like it happened to someone else.

"Good night," the taxi driver says, and I try to think up a way to thank him. I can't move, because how do I leave without paying him? He leans forward and pushes a button. The red alarm clock numbers on his fare counter click to $0.00.

He turns and looks at me with his kind face and his kind eyes, and he nods.

"Good night," he says again. "Be safe."

"Okay, I—I will," I say, like a promise. Like that's how I can thank him.

"The fuck is this?!" Glen says through the intercom when I buzz his apartment, 4C. Deanna looks *pissed* when I get up there. But I can't care.

"You gotta take me home, Dee. You gotta."

I stand there like an island as she skitters around grabbing her stuff. As Glen goes into the bedroom and **CLICK** shuts the door.

Deanna says nothing to me the whole ride back to Connecticut. I say one thing to her: "Dee, Glen had *alcohol* in his kitchen. Right out on the table! Did you not see it?!"

She flips the radio volume to mega, and when we get to

my house, for the first time ever, she doesn't wait to see if I get in. I stand and watch as her taillights thin out.

One bird sings a note, like he's asking permission for it to be morning. Another answers back. And then they're all awake, thousands of them, calling to each other like a symphony warming up. I sit and watch the sky shift from navy to purple to pink.

I feel weird again. I don't know if my Prozac stopped working, but I just—I don't feel right.

We watched this movie in English, *One Flew Over the Cuckoo's Nest*. It's about this guy who gets locked up in a mental hospital, even though there's nothing wrong with him. He's trapped in there with this staff lady who *hates* him, this quiet demon named Nurse Ratched. She tries and tries to make him break—to admit that he's bad, that everything's his fault—but he won't give in. So she has his brain snipped in half. Fucking lobotomy.

It flipped me out, the movie. I sat in the back of class and hyperventilated. I must have been crying too, because my face was all wet, even my shirt. And I keep having nightmares about it. Except in my nightmares, there are no windows.

Deanna hasn't called me in a month. And she hasn't come to school. There's nothing to do without her. There's nobody to talk to. I miss her. I miss my friend.

But it's all my own fault. She tried to hook me up with cute guys who liked me, so we could be matched sets of boyfriends and girlfriends. She tried to make it so we could be with each other, plus guys, all the time. I fucked it up by being a prude.

It's all because I wouldn't let those guys have sex with me.

Not having sex is the stupidest thing I've ever done.

Now I'm paying the price. I'm alone again.

He resurfaces at Club 12 for an 8:30 Thursday meeting. I'm already in my spot on the back counter when the meeting starts, because I was here for the 7:00 meeting too. If I can get the car, I'll camp out at Club 12 meetings all day.

He comes in, says hi to some people, and gets a cup of coffee before finding a seat. Even though the meeting's started. Even though the speaker's speaking. He doesn't care if he's being rude. He's just that Grant.

Because I'm tucked in the way-back corner, I get to watch him as he does all that. He doesn't think to look back here for me, and why would he? We haven't seen each other in a year—a whole year.

Some lady sitting by the coffee moves her bag off a chair. Grant winks at her and sits. He's taking a sip from his

Styrofoam cup, looking around the room, when he spots me. I'm leaning forward so my hair hides my face—like I'm so into the speaker, I can't even notice him—but still, I feel him see me. It's like getting zapped by a cow prod.

I can't, can't, can't seem like I give a shit. That's what made him drop me: letting him see that I was dying to be in his world. I keep my eyes off him for the whole meeting. It's the longest ninety minutes of my life.

At the end of the meeting, everybody holds hands and put their heads down for the Lord's Prayer. And I get this idea: squeeze the hands of the guys on either side of me at "Amen." Like I'm saying, "Thanks, keep coming back," you know? And it works. They both stick around to talk to me, even though I've never seen them before. So instead of loner girl desperate to talk to Grant, I look like popular girl who doesn't know he exists.

When the guys turn to leave, it's like the clouds parting to reveal the face of God. One guy moves left, one guy moves right, and there's Grant, leaning on the wall across from me. His arms are folded over his chest like, I'll wait till the clowns clear out.

You know how, when a cartoon guy sees a foxy lady, his heart jumps out and his eyes go **boi-oi-oing** as his tongue flaps down to the sidewalk? That's me when I see Grant standing there, *waiting*. For me. Family-crest Grant.

It's cold, and his Suburban is parked closest to the door,

so we climb into it. It smells like family trips to ski chalets. It has an 8-track tape deck. The heater comes on hard and fast.

More than we're talking, we're kissing. Grant with his Southport home and his scholarship to Yale and his GRAN key chain, his "I've still got a girlfriend" and his class, his safety, his money—that's the Grant who is kissing me. And I'm kissing back. A lot. Because this is better than Nutella, better than grilled cheese. This is better than Benetton and Coach bags and a brand-new stereo with detachable speakers. This is *love*.

Grant is on top of me on the bench front seat. He's pushed up above me with one hand on the window, the other on my stomach. He's looking down at my face. He's not smiling. I'm not smiling. He's moving his hand up, and oh my God, she's right. Deanna's right. About the eraser rub over the bra. Oh my God.

He's looking at me, and he scoops his hand around my boob and pushes it out of my bra with an "*Uhhh*." And then he puts his face. On my boob. He rubs his face. On my boob. And it's the softest, scratchiest, hottest, meltiest thing I've ever felt and I *love* him. I *love* him as he sucks hard on my one nip and eraser-nubs the other. Then he switches and he's licking the other through my bra and moving his hand down into my jeans, and I feel like some rabid animal as his fingers slide easily under my waistband. I must be really skinny now, since he doesn't even need to unzip me. And his hand is in me and my head is smacking the door because my toes are pushing off the steering wheel because I feel so fucking *good*.

He pulls his hand out of my jeans so he can turn off the heater 'cause we're boiling. He presses up above me again, panting, looking down at me. And he pops the button on my jeans. While he's looking at me, he unzips my jeans. While he's looking at me. And I mean, he's really *looking* at me, like maybe he's in love too. He leans back and unpops his own jeans and moves a little to get his red plaid boxers free from the front *V* of zipper and jeans, and I know what's under there because I *see* it. I see it pushing the red plaid up into a sideways triangle. I see it, and I'm scared. Because what's going to happen?

Grant mashes his hand down my lips, down my chin, down my neck, down my boobs, down my stomach, down and down, and then up and in. And out and in. And he uses his other hand to tug my jeans and undies down, and mother *fuck* does love feel scary and good, and he moves both hands to my sides and he leans down, and he kisses me and I'm spinning and slipping and Go*d*ing, and he's pushing his boxers against me. But I'm scared, and I say, "No." He's still kissing me and I feel—God—and he's pushing, but it's not soft cotton boxers; it's clay. It's warm Play-Doh. I say, "No," and, "I'm a virgin," but he's pushing, but I say, "No," but he's pushing and I—

I don't say anything.

Because he's here.

He wants to be with me.

Maybe he loves me.

Everything is terrifying.

I want, I need to die.

Except now. Now he's *with* me.

And that's the best drug *ever*.

I can't have him not like me again. He pushes and it hurts and he pushes, he pushes, he pushes, and he falls and he goes, "*GOD.*" He's breathing heavy on my neck. We're not moving. No one's moving. He's panting. I'm holding my breath.

And.

And he pushes up and away. He doesn't look at me. Now he's pushing his boxers into his jeans. So I sit up. I press my legs straight. I pull my jeans up and curve toward the window, so he can't see me put my boob back into its package.

When he turns around to me, I turn toward him, and he kisses me on the cheek. Then I say, "That's *it*? That was *sex*?"

He laughs. "You *sure* you're a virgin? You're too good to be a virgin."

I say, "Really. I'm a virgin."

I don't say, *What does this mean?* I don't say, *Will you keep me around now?*

He says, "Well, I guess you better get home…"

I say, "Shit, I didn't even… Fuck. What time is it? Eleven thirty's my school-night curfew."

He says, "Eleven thirty. You better go."

I say, "Fuck. Okay."

I don't say, *I love you.*

And neither does he.

———————

There's no ringing doorbells at midnight, especially when you haven't talked to your best friend in six weeks. So I stand under Deanna's window and whisper-yell, "*Dee!*" When five tries of that don't work, I switch to throwing little rocks, which makes her light come on. Thank *God.* I see a peachy blur at the window; then it slides up.

"What the *fuck*?" she whisper-yells down to me.

"I know, I'm sorry. But I had to come talk to you," I whisper-yell back.

"I'm fucking *grounded*," she says. "My dad caught me not going to your house on my way into the city."

"Oh. Dee?"

"Yeah."

"I—I think I just lost my virginity."

The floodlights pour on and the front door **THUNK**s open, and there's Dad Fazzini in a gray robe and maroon slippers.

"Go home, Cyndy," he says. He's not whispering.

"Okay, but could I talk to Deanna for a second?"

"Go *home*, Cyndy. Do you know what time it is? Go home."

I look up at Deanna, but all I can see is the blinding bright-bright of the floodlight.

When I get to my house, the car clock says 12:30. I'm an hour past my curfew.

I tiptoe from the garage to the front door. My breath puffs out in front of me like an empty cartoon thought bubble. I hold the jangle of keys still as I slide the house key in the lock, and slowwwly, slowwwwwly, smooth—**click**. Gently, caaarefully, I press the thumb lever down. I push on the door and—**KUNK**. Blocked. She locked me out again. Because tough love.

A gust of hot smell puffs up from under my jacket as I crunch around the house through piled-up old snow. I smell like stale bread and dungeons.

The light is on in my mother's bedroom window. She's still awake, probably reading *Tough Love*, her favorite book. I start with the whisper-yell: "Mom!"

Nothing.

Talking voice: "Ma!" Three times. And nothing.

Almost-yelling voice: "Mom, can I talk to you?"

Nothing, nothing, nothing.

Crying voice: "Mom! Please! Let me in!"

Her light goes out.

I sleep in the garage, in the backseat of her car. It's like a trial run, practice for when I do it with the car actually running.

I've been thinking a lot about this, and here's what I've figured out:

☐ family

☐ sponsor

☐ friends

☑ music

Of all the "support systems," music is the only one that's
legit. It's my fire escape, always ready to carry me to safety
when life is going up in flames. The times I've felt truly bleak
have been when family, friends, or a sponsor have disappeared into thin air. The times I've felt truly high have been
when *I* have disappeared into *music*.

That was maybe the worst part about being in Straight:
they took away my music. *All* music. Except fucking nursery

school songs. But in a way, it makes sense. Straight's a drug rehab, right? And music is my drug. Like, I was addicted to Pink Floyd. If I were to listen to Floyd today? I can't even imagine. My brain would melt. I would be *fucked* up.

Thank God for the escape hatch Mr. Littberger and Club 12 have given me. Since I didn't listen to the Dead before Straight, and Top 40 songs didn't even exist until last week, they're not linked to anything dangerous from my druggie past. Only to school and sober dances. Totally safe. And the home economics teacher is so cool, she plays the Top 40 station during class. She turns it up pretty loud, so we can hear it over the sewing machines. Sometimes, *some*times, school can be okay.

I'm working on my first actual, wearable clothing project. It's a skirt. A tiny black miniskirt, exactly like Deanna's. If I can't hang out with her and borrow hers, I definitely need my own, for when I go to Club 12 for my music fix.

I needed more fabric than I thought to cover the elastic band that holds it up, so the skirt part's really pretty short. And tight. But whatever. I go to the bathroom to put it on, and when I'm sock-foot running back to the full-length mirror in class, I get hit by a bomb. Two kids turn a corner and head straight for me: Joanna Azore, my old best druggie friend, and Kyle McCaffrey, her new best cool-kid friend. Kyle, who could be George Michael's twin, is wearing Levi's with bleached handprints all over them, like invisible fans are grabbing his everything. Joanna is wearing a boss Levi's denim with a sheepskin collar. And I'm wearing a hanky, with a hair elastic holding it up.

Jo and Kyle are walking so close they're a single person, wrapped in a bubble of private jokes. I guess my name is one of those jokes, because Kyle says, "Look," thumbing a thumb at me. And Jo does, and Jo smiles, and Jo laughs. And they float away in their bubble toward the smoking pit.

But when I see myself in the home economics mirror, I could pass for Deanna. So at least there's that.

I'm going to Club 12 tonight. Alone. I don't even care. I can't sit in the house with that envelope taunting me like the telltale fucking heart.

My eyes were already crispy red yesterday when I shuffled from the bus to the mailbox. I'd spent the day weirdly crying out front of the guidance office. I had heard the announcement and was trying to get inside to "meet with available counselors," but I stopped when I saw the picture of him they had taped up in the window. Mack, the happy Deadhead. Mack, the dead Deadhead. I saw his smile, and I lost it. I mean I. Lost. It. It was like the last unbroken crayon from the box getting stepped on.

He'd been driving down that long steep hill to Beacon Falls—he was the first of the Beacon Falls kids to get a license *and* a car—when he swerved to not hit a squirrel. The squirrel lived. His friend in the front seat lived. The tree he plowed into lived. Mack didn't live.

I'm basically an idiot for freaking out. It's not even like we were friends. It's just...he was happy and nice, and he was around, you know? He was around somewhere, out in the smoking pit probably, kicking a hacky sack around. He was maybe the only happy, nice thing in the state of Connecticut. And now he's just...not around. I don't know. I couldn't handle it.

And then, after school, I got to the mailbox. There was exactly one envelope, floating like a cream-colored comet in the big, black emptiness. Floating, because it was too light. Too thin.

I didn't want to touch it, 'cause I knew what it was. I knew what it would say. It would say REJECT. It would say YOUR FATHER AND MOTHER'S COLLEGE DOESN'T WANT YOU. It would say YOU'RE NOT GOOD ENOUGH FOR SMITH.

And I was right. That's exactly what it said.

So I'm going to Club 12. By myself. And I'm parking in a spot far away from where Grant's Suburban was parked last week. I don't even look at that spot. I don't even see it. I just go right in the door and hand over my five and start dancing to the Paula Abdul song they're playing, "Straight Up." It doesn't make me think about how Paula and Deanna are lookalikes, or how much I miss Deanna, or how I saw this video at Shane Gallway's house, or how stupid I felt when I was there. Not really. And when Paula sings, I don't think about if anyone's ever gonna love *me* or how I have no friend, no boyfriend, no sponsor, no nobody to come to Club 12 with. I only have myself, so I don't *think*. I hear and feel and ride the horns and drums with my eyes closed. I dance until I'm gone.

The DJ switches it up, flooding the room with the musical version of a sunset, the synthesizer opening of "Night and Day." I don't know if I'm dancing with Al B. Sure! or *being* him, in my mind, but I see and feel his shiny, curly hair and his thin little mustache and his big, gray, acid-wash jean jacket. I *feel* his ecstatic "*Whoo!*" all down my front, and I'm dancing like he does in the video, when he snaps his fingers and holds his hands in an *O* over his head like a ballerina, then throws them down and open to really make his point.

I'm acting out the lyrics as I dance, and when I run my fingers through my hair, my elbow bonks somebody. I open my eyes and this guy is dancing with me. Like, close enough that I can see his face in the darkness. It has the color and shine of melted candle wax. He has small blue eyes and a mouth that, when he sees me seeing him, doesn't smile. It smirks. I can tell the difference.

He's older; that's obvious from his loafer shoes and his carefully combed hairdo. I want to go back to where I was, back into the song, so I close my eyes again. Al B. is at that part where he's really smooth-swinging it, and this guy puts his arms around me and starts spinning me like we're at a sock hop. And holy shit, it's more fun than a carnival ride. I open my eyes again and smile at him. He smiles instead of smirks this time, and we dance the rest of the song, and it's fucking awesome. Because I'm not alone at this dance anymore. And when you're dancing in this way, where the guy is kind of pushing you around, it feel like you're on wheels. It feels like you have wings.

Then my friend the DJ puts on "Secret Rendezvous," and from the very first drumbeat, this guy is holding my hand and twirling me out and rolling me in and dipping me way, way back in a back bend. I feel like that girl everybody wanted on *Saturday Night Fever*. I feel like the prettiest girl in the room.

We dance that way the rest of the night, four straight hours, without saying a word to each other. When the DJ puts on the last song—a slow jam, Journey, to make everyone feel sleepy—I want to slap him. Because this night cannot end. I can't go back to that house, that envelope, that dead-end-what-now-I'm-trapped crypt. I can't. I won't. I'll drive into the ocean before I'll—

"Let's get out of here." He says those words right next to my ear.

I turn my head and we're almost lip-to-lip. He's wearing

the smirk again. He turns and walks out, so I follow him. Out the door, through the smokers, across the parking lot, past my mother's cop mobile, to a sweet little red sports car. He puts his key in the driver's door like he's about to leave me here, alone with my savage thoughts and poltergeist memories.

"Don't go. Please." The words blast out like diarrhea. I can't stop them, because I don't feel them coming.

He turns back toward me and I can see him way better now in the bright streetlight. He's got a pointy nose and thin lips. He's got wrinkles and small hands. He uses them to pick up both of mine.

"What's your name, beautiful."

"Cyndy?"

"Mine's Damien. Get in."

He slides into the driver's seat, turns on the engine, and revs it. I race around to the passenger side, so he won't leave without me. And we go back to not talking as I close myself into his car. He punches it into reverse. He skates backward a little, then rockets into drive—shift-shift-jerk—and we're out of the parking lot, around the curve, and sizzling onto Post Road.

It feels like I should've had to tell somebody I was leaving. I should've had to say bye to someone when I left the club. But to who? There's nobody. Nobody knows I was there, nobody knows I left.

The car is vapor locked, tight as a spaceship. Nothing outside can get in, and nothing inside can get out. We're sealed in here with bass and drums and speed as we leave the world behind, screaming through red lights and past dark storefronts and skidding a hard left into the woods, where it's hills and curves and dark, headlights showing, then hiding, the tall thread of trees and nothing else. Where are we?

Damien pushes a new tape into the stereo and Information Society's sharp chemical sounds take over the oxygen and my heartbeat. I don't have to be dancing to escape. I can be in a fast car with loud music to forget everything. When the acid beat of "What's on Your Mind" takes over the speakers, my seat is throbbing and he's shifting and pushing the car faster and higher, and I need to scream or explode because my skin can't contain me. If he could hear me, I'd beg him to *please* keep driving fast and hard and loud like this forever.

And he does. He drives and drives for the whole album, and it's ecstasy until he jerks the car into a dark driveway and stops.

"Where are we?"

"Weston," he says. He switches off the car and gets out, so I do too.

Weston is quiet. Weston is dark. Weston is rich. Weston is far.

"Um…what're we doing here?"

"It's two o'clock in the morning. I'm tired."

That's his whole answer. He opens a door and goes in the house.

But I don't. I stand there in my home economics skirt and my black pumps and my freezing bare arms, and my thoughts come back. They come back like, *Where the fuck am I?*

And like, *Weston, idiot.*

And like, *Yeah, but* why *am I here?*

And like, *Because you're fucking stupid.*

And like, *But it felt so good! It was so fun! I needed an escape!*

And like, *Every party's gotta end.*

And like, *So what do I do now?*

And like,

And like, *Hello? Help?*

And like,

He's turned lights on in the house, so I can see everything, because the house is made of all windows. It reminds me of this movie my mother loved when I was younger. *Sleeper*, it was called. Woody Allen was the only human in this outer-space future world, and everybody was out to get him, but he didn't know why. He only knew he had to be scared all the time.

I go up to the door and knock, which seems stupid and weird. Then I open the door and go, "Hello?" which also seems stupid and weird.

He appears in the doorway leading to the next room, wearing, swear to God, a paisley silk robe.

"What are you doing out there, sitting zazen?" he asks.

"Ummm…could you…could you take me back to Club 12?"

"Tomorrow I will. I'm tired," he says, and goes into the other room. The light in that room goes off.

I've never seen a taxi in Weston. I've never seen a taxi anywhere in Connecticut. I reach my hand in my bag to feel for my car keys, to know I'll be able to get myself home. Just, tomorrow. To know I'll be fine. Tomorrow.

There's a little **thump-thump** behind me, and a cat starts rubbing against my legs. Cats are good. Cats are safe. She lets me pet her once, then she walks out of the room. So I follow her. She leads me to a bedroom. Where he's lying in a bed.

"I, um…" I say from the doorway.

"I know. I'm not going to try anything. Remember me saying I was tired? I meant that. Come on." He pats the bed. "You're safe."

The cat jumps up next to him, which seems like a sign. So I step out of my pumps and lie down on the far-far-away-from-him edge of the bed. Because it's like 3:00 a.m. now. And I got myself into this. And I don't have a way out.

He turns off the light and turns over on his side with his back toward me. The kitty comes up and pushes her face against mine. I pet her. She purrs. His breaths go deep and even. I guess he wasn't lying. I guess I'm really safe.

I fall asleep knowing my mother's house is double locked.

I fall asleep in a bed, not in a car's backseat. I fall asleep with my hand in soft kitty fur.

I wake up with him on top of me. "Damien." His face is even whiter, even waxier, in the daylight. He's not kissing me. He's not looking at me. But he's touching me. Hard. He's squeezing my boobs like they're not-ripe-enough fruit and he's mad about it. He's ripping my stockings to get them open. He's holding me down by the shoulders. I'm trying to go Hulk. I'm trying to get him off me. But I can't.

He pushes himself against me down there, where he tore my stockings. And it hurts. It feels like a brick. I'm crying and telling him, "I'm not! I'm scared! I only—*stop!*"

He doesn't look at me. He doesn't listen. He doesn't stop. He holds me in place with an arm bone across my shoulders, my neck; he holds himself up with his hand hard-squeezing my fruit. And he bricks me. He breaks me. I stop trying to fight him and I go away. I go away. I'm forgetting this already.

I come out of my trance when he slams his car door. We're at the Club 12 parking lot. There's a Volvo full of people in the spot next to us. I get out of his sweet little red sports car. He's leaning into the trunk and then he's standing back up, holding a pair of ice skates.

"You guys are going skating?" I say around all the desperation, the scared, the please-please-please in my throat.

"Yup," he says.

"Can I go?" I ask.

"Nope," he says.

He gets into the Volvo, which backs out and drives away. And I stand there with cold wind blowing into the ripped-open hole in my stockings.

Maybe I'm stupid, maybe I'm crazy, but when my mother's gross boyfriends come over, I am *not* staying in that house. And going to meetings doesn't cut it anymore. At meetings, you quietly examine your feelings. At sober dances, you loudly escape them. I've done enough examining for one lifetime.

So I'm back at Club 12 with a plan. I'm not looking at anybody. I'm not talking to anybody. I'm not even wearing a skirt, okay? I'm wearing jeans and sneakers. And I'm dancing. Nothing else. Just dancing.

But when I go outside to take a breath of moon, *ping!* There's a guy at my side. Dark hair, fancy jacket. Mean eyes.

"Hi," he says, moving in and caging me between his body and the car I was leaning on. "My name's Jacob."

"Hi." I tilt my head back from him, like, *No thanks, Jacob.*

"What a neck," he says. "I wish I was a vampire."

"Um, yeah," I say, snapping my head back and smashing my chin into the flat bone over my boobs. "I, ah—I gotta get back inside. My friend's waiting."

"What, I'm not your friend?" he says, putting his other hand down on the car roof. I'm trapped in a prison of Jacob.

"Yeah, ha. Actually…" I pull my keys out and jingle them, even though it's not even eleven. "I gotta be getting home."

I go to duck under his arm, but he catches me under the chin and lifts and pushes me back against the car. He's leaning in to kiss me and I go, "*No!*" Like, loud.

He puts the brakes on his face, stopping a half inch from mine. "Damien told me about you," he whispers. His face looks like Jacque's used to before he'd hit me. "You're a little slut."

He lifts his arm and I run, I *run*, to my mother's car. I don't look in the rearview as I'm leaving, even though I know this is goodbye to Club 12. Didn't those kids know they could never return to Narnia? Weren't they all torn up about it too?

I make as much noise as I can coming back into the house. Whatever my mother and her boyfriend are doing, I wanna give them plenty of time to stop. But they're just watching TV, I guess, because when I yell, "Hi! I'm home!" my mother calls back from the family room.

"Oh, there's my beautiful daughter! Come here, Cyndy. Let me introduce you to my friend."

I have to say hello if I ever want to use the car again. I walk into the room, and smile, and say hi, and block my ears as my mother says, "She's eighteen now. Isn't she gorgeous?" I turn and walk out and thank God I'm in jeans, not a skirt, as I feel the boyfriend's eyes go down my back to my butt.

When I get to my room, I turn the volume all the way up on my phone/alarm clock/radio, but I can't drown out my brain. I pray to God, but he doesn't stop my thoughts. My thoughts about how Jacob was going to hit me because I didn't do what I was supposed to. Which was to be a good girl and do what the man says.

I should know by now that that's my sacred duty. I've been learning that lesson since I was in kindergarten, when my mother married Jacque. When he started making me lay down for him. When my mother let it happen because she knows the rules. Because she doesn't fight. Because maybe she *gave* me to *get* something for herself.

And then, when I got old enough to fight back, I got hit. And when I ran away, I got locked up. And that was part of the lesson too. Because that's not the way it works. Girls don't fight. Girls don't win. Girls are a pretty, sparkly lure at the end of the fishing line—*Look at my gorgeous teen daughter!*—used to bring men closer. Men with their money and their hands. Once the men are lured, the girl has to give them what they want. Because that's all girls are good for.

For—

For—

For *sex*.

That's it.

Those are the rules, so how *dare* I fight back. How *dare* I say no. If I had just done what I was supposed to, everything would have been so easy.

It doesn't matter that there are things I want. Like, just to be around somebody. To have somebody want to be around me. To dance or listen to music or go for a ride or go ice skating. Doesn't matter if I want that, because my wants don't count. Only boy-wants count. So if *they* want to go for a ride and listen to music with me, I get lucky. But if they want something else, I have two choices: lay flat or get punished.

This doesn't seem right. And maybe it isn't right. But this is the way it is for me if I don't want to be alone. Or get hit.

These are the kinds of thoughts I can't stop. These, and thoughts about how stupid I was to send Steven Ross a stupid heart. Like he'd be happy to know I just…*liked* him. No wonder he never frigging called me.

I sit on my floor with my head pressed to the phone/alarm clock/radio speaker, trying to stop my thoughts. It's a long, long night.

———

"I—I think I need to go back to the psychiatrist," I tell the guidance counselor, but she seems a little distracted. She was putting her key in her office door when I came in; now she's sitting but still wearing her big winter coat.

"Have you told your mother?" she asks, leaning away from me to put her lunch bag in her desk drawer.

"Have *I*? No. It doesn't work like that."

"Well, that would be the first step, Cyndy. Especially since you're eighteen. You're not a minor anymore, so I can't act on your behalf."

"What?"

Her phone starts ringing. She picks up with her right hand while shrugging her left out of her coat.

"Right, I know. Late start this morning. See you in a sec," she says into the phone.

I can take a hint.

"I'm sorry, Cyndy," she says, as I stand and open her door. "I wish there was more I could do. Talk to your mom, okay?"

Her phone starts ringing again as I close the door behind me.

Sometimes, when my mother's at work, I use her bathroom. And when I use her bathroom, I read the *Guideposts* magazines she keeps by the toilet. And when I sit on the toilet and read *Guideposts*, I get little messages from God. That's where I was when I got this one:

WHEN GOD CLOSES A DOOR, HE OPENS A WINDOW.

So that's what I did. I got up off the toilet and opened the window. It's like the birds were out there waiting for me, because they started swooping and singing, and I swear, they were talking to me. Not in English, exactly, but—I don't know how to explain. Just, I suddenly understood some things, as I stood there watching and listening to them.

They were so happy, arcing back and forth like hacky sacks. They reminded me of Mack. Who's dead. Who shouldn't be dead but who *is* dead. The birds told me I didn't want to be dead. They told me that inside, underneath what's happening on the surface, I'm like Mack; I'm like them. Happy for no reason. And it's not right to kill what's happy. Even if the happy isn't showing yet.

So I decided, again, not to die. Kind of for Mack. Kind of for the birds. Kind of for me. I decided, instead, to tell my mother that she needs to take me back to the psychiatrist. That I can't wait for my six-month-dosage evaluation; I need to go *now*. I even made the appointment myself, so my mother couldn't pretend to forget to do it.

She was pissed. As she told me in the car on the way there. "Do you have *any* idea how much you're costing me right now? Just the gas to drive to this appointment alone is—"

But I did something unbelievable: I cut her off. I reached through the space between us, clicked on the radio, and turned it up, loud. If you don't believe in miracles yet, you will now. The song that was playing? The Grateful Dead. The one where he tells us, over and over, that he's gonna survive.

Which is so true. The song *and* the message from God about closing doors and opening windows. Because Blanca's been here all along, a window locked tight. All I had to do was close the door on Club 12, and **fwoosh!** The Blanca window opens, and all this fresh air rushes in.

Here's how it happens. I'm shuffling into school Monday, gripping my scungy Dunkin' mug. I'm late-late, as usual. But this semester, my first class is math with Mr. Gomez, and he doesn't think late arrival is cute. So whenever I click open the door and try to smile my way to my seat, he's always, "No thanks, Etler. Go sign in at the office." Which means detention.

Monday, though, when I see Blanca walking toward his class on her way back from the lav, I'm like, "Blanca! Sneak me in!"

And she smiles and goes, "I gotcha."

So *she* clicks the door open, and *she* smiles at Mr. Gomez, and when he looks back down at his grading, she finger curls at me and I slip into the room behind her. One door click, two students, no Gomez the wiser. After we slide our butts into our seats, Blanca turns around and gives me a thumbs-up. Which feels, swear to God, as good as "Welll…*hey!*"

The next day, before English class, Blanca and Candy McAllister are talking about college rejection letters. Blanca turns to me and asks, "Where'd you apply, Cyndy?"

And I say, "Smith."

And Candy says, "Only?"

And I say, "Only."

And Blanca says, "Accepted?"

And I say, "Rejected."

And Blanca says, "Ouch."

And I say, "Ouch."

The weird thing is, this conversation about getting rejected makes me feel accepted.

"What'd you do when you got the letter?" Candy asks.

"I went out dancing."

Which makes them both laugh.

"You're such a trip, Etler," Blanca says.

"Not the acid kind, though," I say. And they both laugh even harder. Which feels better than a hug.

Then Mrs. Skinner comes in the room. She looks at the three of us talking, and she tilts her head and smiles. And suddenly everything's okay, like the first day of spring.

Mrs. Skinner says to copy the notes from the board, but Blanca writes me a note instead. It says, "I'm going dancing Saturday. You in?"

On a little slip of paper I write back,

OH

MY

GOD

FUCK

YES

She reads it, then turns and gives me another thumbs-up. Blanca Halliwell. The cheerleader. With the perfect blond curly hair. Oh my God, fuck yes.

To get to Blanca's club, we take the Merritt, not 95. The Merritt's a whole other world, more trees than traffic. We get off at an exit for Greenwich, but didn't we just drive by a "Welcome to New York" sign? In the dark, I couldn't tell. Blanca's got the sunroof open and a new wave mix tape playing, so we can't really talk. Which is awesome. Because what could I talk about with a cheerleader?

Before I got in her car, she had said, "I like your outfit," which made me feel great. It's a mishmash, my outfit: Guess jeans, black pumps I got from Deanna, and a sweatshirt I sliced up to look *Flashdance*. Then, when Blanca was curving the car around the exit ramp, I think she said, "I'm psyched you came out." Which made me feel delirious, but also mortified. Because who thinks in words like "delirious"? And who gets delirious about having a new friend?

Her club is a black box in a black parking lot surrounded by black woods. It's called the Haven, even though there's no sign. She pushes the black door open, and there are a few people in a hallway and a door guy who says, "Age?" and Blanca says, "Eighteen." She gives him a ten and he gives her a turquoise wristband.

He says to me, "Age?" and I ask, "Why?" and he says, "Twenty-one and up to drink."

I look at Blanca with my stomach doing somersaults. "Drink?"

She says, "Just give him a ten." So I do, and he gives me a turquoise wristband.

The next thing I know, we're in the black cubicle of the club. There are zero windows, and there's a bar with glass shelves and fluorescent lights and bottles. I'm scared. Because no windows. Because alcohol. Because it's half Straight, half everything Straight warned me about. Because what am I doing here? Because what if alcohol spills on me? What if I slip and have a drink? What if Blanca realizes what a loser I am?

I'm spinning in a tornado of fear. I can't be here with all this alcohol, but I can't get home on my own! If I ask Blanca to drive me home, she'll never talk to me again, like Deanna. I'll be back to zero friends. But I can't endanger my sobriety! But—but—but then these needles of sound shoot out of the speakers with these soft, fast drums behind them. They pierce me and thump me, and everyone's going to the dance floor and moving together with their heads down. Every angel in Heaven's going *aaaaaaahh* down a big, metal tunnel and all of this sound—all the needles and drums and Heaven—it's all tangled together. I'm not worried about anything anymore. I'm in a cradle and everyone else is too. We're all wrapped together in this soft, sharp, drum tunnel sound. Everything makes sense—the way I'm moving, the way they're moving, the tanging cowbell from the left speaker, the whip-crack from the right.

The song fades out like the last gift under the Christmas tree. You grab it all excited, but the tag has your sister's name on it.

"What was *that*?" I ask Blanca.

"'Blue Monday,'" she says back.

"Blue, as in depressed?" I ask, louder, because the next song is rolling in like migrating birds.

"Bingo," she says.

She's dancing now, her hands swirling around in front of her, looking like no Blanca I've ever seen at school. So I keep my next question in my head. But...everybody in here danced to a song about...depression? Like, *every*body? So maybe...maybe I'm not the only one who gets that way?

This song is beautiful and gentle and kind, and everybody who's dancing has on this soft smile, like they have honey on their tongues. The drums roll upward and the singer belts it out from the back of his throat, sing-yelling how it's *his* life. *His*.

How have I never heard this music before? This must be the stuff that made Deanna jump from MTV to VH1 or vice versa when it came on. "Soft stuff. Gross," she'd say, jabbing at the clicker like she wanted to break a nail.

The next song starts like a marching army. Blanca goes to sit, so I follow her.

She sings along, grinning like she's in on the joke. I hope I don't look as awestruck as I feel, but what did I just walk into? They're selling alcohol and stomping and laughing? What the *fuck*, I'm here with a *cheer*leader? I should be fucking terrified. But I'm not. I actually feel safer than I ever knew I could.

Some kids walk up to say hi to Blanca, but I can't see them because I'm blinded by the one. The boy, tucked in the back of their group. The one glowing like a night-light. I force myself to turn and watch the people dancing, but then Blanca—my own personal Jesus—grabs my hand and pulls me into their circle.

"This is Cyndy, my friend from school," she says. "She's practically an anarchist."

Her friends don't ask her what the fuck she's talking about, or if she has *any* idea what I'm really like inside. Instead, they smile and nod. All but the glow boy. Glow boy moves toward me and puts out his hand out, but kind of low, like he's not assuming I want to shake it.

"I'm Seth," he says. I put my hand in his. It's soft, and it's warm, and—does it *have* to hurt when you get electrocuted? Because that's how it feels, touching Seth's hand. Like getting soft, warm electrocuted.

I let go of his hand and sit back, because I don't know what else to do. Glow boy stands there, semi-behind his friends. A new song starts, so sweet, with the sound of waves swishing in. Everything's fine. I'm here, and everybody's here, but it feels like there's nobody here at all, because nobody is staring

at me. Nobody wants anything from me. We're all just...
here. Together.

I lean over to Blanca and ask, "What's this place called
again?"

"The Haven," she says.

The Haven. One *e* away from Heaven.

33

APRIL 1990
THREE YEARS AND ONE MONTH OUT

I'm in a car that's driving fast and blasting music again, but this time, the car's being driven by a girl. And this time, it's 8:00 a.m. on a school day. And this time, I know where we're going. New York. Me and Blanca. Swear to God.

She's playing another mix tape, but this time it's all one band: Pet Shop Boys. They're the most delicious thing I've ever heard. We've got the sunroof open and the windows closed, so we have air rush *and* music. I've got my hands up in the wind and my ear pressed to a speaker. The beat is rolling as fast as the tires, and this man—this sad, sad man who still somehow kept living—is singing about how everything he is and does, all of it's a sin. It's tragic and happy all at once. It's thrilling and heartbreaking and scrambled and hopeful. I could fucking *live* in this music.

The next song starts with the tick of a cotton-wrapped second hand, staggered by the **THUMP-THUMP** of slow-approaching feet. Something's coming, something bad, but then these tender violins are pulling a blanket over you and tucking in the edges, so it's okay. You're okay. And he starts singing about wanting to put a gun to your own head.

Wait. The Pet Shop Boys have felt that way? And they're *telling* us about it? Instead of doing suicide, they make gorgeous *music* about it?

When Blanca ejects the tape to flip it, I can't keep my thoughts to myself. "I never knew this stuff. Where did you *find* it?"

"What do you mean, 'find'? This is old! It came out almost five years ago! Where have *you* been?"

Luckily she pushes the B side in, so I don't have to try to answer that question.

We spend the day doing unbelievable things: trying on gowns in Saks Fifth Avenue, looking at the hoi polloi through the windows of Tavern on the Green, riding the merry-go-round in Central Park. It's like we're in our own *Ferris Bueller's Day Off*. It's like I'm a normal, laughing teenager. When we go by the pond with the rowboats stacked outside, I get a little sad that Deanna's not my friend anymore. But only a little. And when I tell Blanca about that night, about being stuck in the pond with no paddle, she starts laughing. So I start laughing. And suddenly I get what the Pet Shop Boys songs are saying. You can have sad but still be happy. You can have both at the same time.

On the drive home, I'm digging through Blanca's backseat junk for another tape she wants to play me, and my fingers sweep through a pile of crackles. Her pompom. I turn back front and hold it up, this whisper-light red-and-white winner's trophy. I know it's wicked ballsy, but I shake it. I can't not.

"I *love* this," I say.

"My pom?" she asks, in the same tone as, "I know, right?"

"I've always wanted to be a cheerleader," I tell her.

"You? Seriously?" she says. As if my desperation to be her isn't so obvious, you could see it from outer space.

"Oh my God, yes. Always."

"Well, fucking come on! We need an extra for all the end-of-year events, since Ashley broke her leg and Candace moved away. We can't do our routines with a girl missing."

"Nuh-uh. Seriously? Me?"

"Seriously! Can you yell? Uh-huh. Can you jump? I'm sure. Can you look good in a short skirt? Hell yes. So fucking why not?"

I can't say anything, because if I opened my mouth, all the confetti'd bits of my heart would come spraying out. Instead, I shake her pompom in time with Depeche Mode.

———

We're back at the Haven, and I'm having this…experience. The music has found the fault line in my brain, and my psyche is, like, detonating.

I'm standing in a corner, trying to be invisible. Trying to close off my front and sides, so no one can sneak up on me, so I can 100 percent focus on the people, the dancing, the whatever it is that makes this place so *nice*. I'm leaning on a chest-high speaker when this song comes on faintly, like the gentle fingertips of Jesus on a lamb. A violin starts and someone presses piano keys, one at a time. A voice matching the violin comes in, lungs wide open in a cry, a question directed at God.

Whhhhhhhy?

The violin-voice describes a kid who's kicked around, who's laughed at by everyone. Then it delivers a hard, sharp truth: the kid's not gonna find any love at home. Not ever. This song's about me.

My brain blasts apart and clicks back together. I understand now: everything Straight taught me, everything my mother said, it was all a lie. I'm not a bad kid who made her mother's husband touch her, who ran away to be a druggie. I'm a sad kid who made too much noise when life hurt. Who ran away to try to make it stop.

I can't cry at the Haven. I need to not cry at the Haven. I need to think about the next song as it stutters in, a distorted heartbeat. This searing song, it tells me I'm human, and that *every*one needs to feel loved. The Haven takes over my brain again and I get it. We *all* do. We all need the same fucking thing, and we'll try and try and try until we find it. We just—we just all need to feel loved.

I leave my spot at the speaker and blend into the moving crowd. I'm like them, and they're like me. I'm not a druggie whore. I'm not. They're not. We're all just kids. Dancing. Needing love. A cage full of doves breaks open inside my chest. I'm flying and I'm dancing and I feel okay. I feel so okay.

When I lift my head and shake my hair out of my eyes I see Blanca, sitting in a chair and talking to that glow boy, Seth. They're beautiful. A beautiful song is playing. The world feels like it makes sense, like everybody's doing what they should, to get what they really need.

The glow boy looks up at me and smiles. His face gives me this light, free feeling, like seeing the "Welcome to Florida!" sign after a long drive in a stuffy car.

34

Mrs. Skinner has us write a reflective essay today to practice for the SATs. Here's the question that was on the chalkboard when we came in the room:

What is the most important element of a successful life, and what have you learned in your high school career about how to obtain that vital element?

I'm gonna have to plead the fifth if they ask me to read this one out loud. I don't even know if I can let Mrs. Skinner read it. I might have to give her a second draft after I heavily revise. But here's draft one.

Love and Cookies

There is one ingredient every life needs, in the same way that every cookie needs flour. That one ingredient is love. No flour? No cookie. No love? No life.

Love has different nicknames, including *popularity*, *acceptance*, and *boyfriend.* I have tried different tricks in my attempts to get each of them, and I have learned a lot in the process.

I started, at a young age, with my mother. She was really distracted, so it took a lot of work. Over the years I tried gluing myself to her, asking her questions, apologizing when she was in a bad mood, blaming everything that went wrong on myself, and telling her, "I love you." I just recently realized that some people don't find love at home.

I also tried to get love from relatives when I was around them. My ploy there was to tell them how much I liked being with them. That was a flop too. They liked my older sister instead of me, even though she was just *there*, doing what they did. That lesson, I guess, is that blending in will get you accepted, but being excited won't.

When I realized I wasn't going to find my place

with family, I found a place with a new friend,
Joanna. With Jo, I actually got in. She really
accepted me, which then got me semi-accepted
by her very cool guy friends. But to get in, I had
to do some bad stuff. I smoked pot a couple
times. And some other things I don't really want
to describe here. I got so in I had hope for having
love from real friends. I got so much hope I ran
away from my mother's house and husband. But
running away put an end to *that* love because it
got me signed in to Straight.

Straight is the tough-love drug rehab where I
spent sixteen months. It was even harder trying
to scrape out love at Straight. To be honest,
everything I tried there failed. It took a long,
scary time to stop being, like, brutalized every
day. Eventually I learned to believe what they told
me about myself and to play by every single tiny
rule. My reward wasn't love. It was more like
finally being left alone. So I learned playing by the
rules may get you something, but it won't be love.

When I was in Straight, I got to hear about
how other kids tried to get love themselves.
They cut school or did vandalism to be part of
the cool crowd. They blew pot smoke in their
dogs' faces to make their friends laugh. They put

drugs in their butt holes and took buses across the country to help their drug dealer boyfriends. They had sex with grown men to get money to buy drugs for their friends. Everybody did this crazy stuff, and when their parents showed up at Straight, they yelled, "I love you, Mom and Dad!" but their parents never said "I love you" back. This tells me people will do anything, anything, to feel loved. Especially when their parents don't love them.

Once I got out of Straight, I tried finding love with different boys. My tricks included going along with whatever they wanted, sending a nice present, being really quiet, and dancing. All of these approaches seemed, for a high, sparkling minute, like they were going to work. In that sparkling minute, I had euphoria like no drug could ever give me. But my high ended when I said I wasn't ready for sex. Then the boy either quit wanting to be around me or he took sex anyway. I hope the lesson I'm getting from this turns out wrong, but the lesson seems to be boys only want girls for sex. So if a girl wants love, she's not going to get it from a boy.

Nowadays I try to get love from God—which sometimes works and sometimes doesn't. I'm rolling

out my new plan, which is to become a cheerleader. Cheerleaders are always surrounded by
friends, and they always have a boyfriend. So it
seems like this plan might be the winner.

Cookies need flour, and humans need love. I
used to eat and eat and eat cookies thinking they
could be a replacement for love. I learned that
doesn't work. I've learned a whole lot of other
things that don't work too. I can't say I know yet
what *does* work to get love, but luckily for me,
I have two whole months left of high school to
figure it out.

I think I might really be onto something with this cheerleader idea. I mean, there are two things in life that everybody adores: babies and cheerleaders. If I can get on the
squad with Blanca and learn what I'm doing, maybe I can
become a college cheerleader! The only thing I'm worried
about is, to be a cheerleader, you have to be mean. Like
Tiffani Malta. You have to be able to smile on the sidelines
when the whole world's looking at you, then look super-
pissed the rest of the time, so everyone knows you're better
than them. Or like Blanca, who's not mean but walks around
chisel faced, never smiling. I don't think a cheer-face can
be like mine, always stupid smiling, even when it's about
to cry. And I don't know if cheerleaders can be the type of

people who give bananas to bums. Isn't it a prerequisite of cheerleading to be kind of a bitch?

But maybe not. Because Candy McAllister's not a bitch. She totally smiles. For example, she smiled at me when she asked to use my eraser. And she spends her study hall with the special-ed kids by choice. And she can't think she's better than everyone else, because her hair is all crispy and it's got dark roots. So maybe you *can* be a cheerleader if you're not bitch-perfect.

Anyway, I can't be that far off from cheerleader material because Cheerleader Blanca and me are going back to the Haven tomorrow night. She totally wouldn't be hanging out with me if I wasn't in her league-ish, right?

Blanca was walking around thinking I was out of *her* league. I swear. She pretty much tells me so on the ride to the Haven.

She starts out like, "Listen, I'm really sorry about Mack."

I don't even ask why she's saying sorry. I just go, "Can you believe? God. All the Beacon Falls kids must be so crippled."

"But you especially. I mean, wasn't he like…"

"Like what? Blanca! You think I had *sex* with *Mack*?!"

"No! No, but wasn't he like, a brother to you? Wasn't he the one who got you to quit shooting heroin and get help?"

"Shooting *her*oin? Blanca, what? No way! *Her*oin? God, I barely even smoked a joint! What are *you* smoking? I never even had a conversation with Mack. His friends were the *druggie*-druggies. Where did you get *that* idea?"

She doesn't say anything for like a whole minute. Then she goes, "So you *weren't* shooting smack?"

"Oh my *God*, no! I was terrified to even toke a joint!"

"Then how come everybody's saying you're like, this serious badass? Fuck. Never mind."

I try to see her face, but it's too dark. I can only see her outline. She's in the shape of a balloon that got its air leaked out.

Blanca doesn't care that I go right to my corner by the speaker instead of sitting with her. That's okay, though. I like this corner. It feels like the safest little space in a safe big space. But after a couple songs, I'm distracted. It's glow boy. It's Seth. He's standing there talking to Blanca again, but he's looking right at me.

His smile pulls me over, and he says hi, and I say hi, and Blanca might still be sitting here, but I stop seeing her. He holds up a hand which is weird, because didn't we just say hi?—and he taps on his bracelet. Which is red, not turquoise. Which means he's allowed to buy alcohol.

He leans toward me, lighting me up with the glow, and goes, "My friend got me this! Want a beer?"

He asks me that like I'm normal. Like I'm Wendi or Mia or any other untainted, unbroken girl who could say, "Yeah!" He has no idea that I live in a sobriety cage, that I'm only allowed out on a leash with a choke collar.

If I could say, "Yeah!" I'd be that free girl, that fun girl, that girl everybody loves. Because *that's* the secret door to popularity: alcohol. Seriously. Who are the loser girls nobody wants to talk to? Me, plus the science geeks who don't even *have* to Just Say No, because they're never in a social situation. And who are the chicks everyone wants to sit with at lunch? The cheerleaders, like Blanca, who are at every keg party. And the stoners, like Joanna. Even Deanna, the one other sober kid, who's fine with her boyfriend having booze right out on the table. I may be human and need to be loved, but I never will be if I keep being the anti-alcohol freakazoid.

A little throat clear snaps me out of my manipulative druggie thoughts. It's Blanca, who's been sitting between Seth and me the whole time. She looks at me like, *Dude, really?* and she's right. What the fuck am I thinking?

"No, I'm good. Thanks," I say to Seth, and look back at Blanca to make sure we're cool. She gives a tiny nod, but still. Her usual not-smile looks like an actual frown all of a sudden.

"How 'bout a Coke?" Seth asks, as if that's a normal question. As if perfect, unsmiling Blanca isn't sitting right in front of him. As if he really, for some reason, wants to do something nice for me.

"Okay, yeah," I say without even thinking to say, *Diet.* Without wondering how I'll get home tonight, since Blanca stood up and walked out. Without trying to figure out how this is even happening to me. The glow feels so good, it erases all my thoughts.

I stand in a trance until Seth comes back from the bar. He's carrying two big red plastic cups: one with un-diet Coke for me and one with frigging beer, for him. I better pray to God to keep me from freaking out. I have un-diet Coke and *alcohol* in my face, *by my own choice*. But I don't actually need to pray, because somehow I feel all right. Like, confident, even. It makes no sense, but I feel 100 percent okay.

We keep pulling our chairs closer and closer to try to hear each other, and finally Seth goes, "Do you want to go outside?" I nod, and he picks up my cup for me and steps back to let me go first.

Outside there's a different kind of music: crickets singing, leaves clicking, breeze shushing. Since there's no I-95 next door like at Club 12, it's a nature soundtrack. Plus Seth. Plus me.

When he's talking, I feel this pull. I want to put my hands on his skin. I don't do it, but I want to. And what the fuck?

I tell him I live in Monroe with my mother and little sister. I tell him I want to be a cheerleader, and I *really* want to be a writer. I tell him I don't know where I'm going for college and that that's kind of scary. I don't tell him about my mother's ex-husband or about Straight. I let him think I'm normal.

He tells me he lives in Newtown. He tells me he works at Macy's. He tells me he got promoted to the whites department, so now he sells satin sheets. He says, "Don't laugh. I know it's cheesy."

Here are the reasons he's *so* not my type:

1. His hair is spikey. It's got, like, guy gel in it.
2. He's wearing Z. Cavaricci jeans, with the angled pockets. The fucking anti–Levi's.
3. I think he's got *cologne* on.

It's almost kind of embarrassing. If the Deadheads in the smoking pit saw me talking to a guy in Z. Cavaricci, they'd laugh bullet holes right through me. But the glow cancels out all that.

We talk and talk, and when we get to the *Rocky Horror Picture Show*—he's seen it too—he puts his cup down, and he puts my cup down. He puts his palms against mine, which makes the whole circuit board of my brain light up. He presses his hands upward, taking mine with them, and our wrists press together and our arm bones press together and our elbows and upper arms, and we're face-to-face, and his breath smells like beer. Like *beer!* And then we're kissing. I'm kissing fucking *beer.* It's like that Starburst commercial where a tidal wave of color knocks everything down and flings it back up in shivering splashes. It's like *that.* We're kissing and smiling at the same time, our arms pressed together over our heads. I'm the highest, happiest normal girl who ever flew, until Seth pulls back and my mind snaps into place: *Beer!* Beer! *I have beer, in my mouth!*

I pull away and grab my cup of un-diet Coke and take one single, sweet sip to clean out my mouth. That was a beer kiss! Was that—was that a slip? Did I just go back to drinking and drugging? *And* un-dieting? *God*, am I gonna—

Glow boy cuts my spin by touching me again. Just my hand. In his hand. I look up from my cup, which I was staring into, and he's looking at my palm. Not my boobs, not my lips. My palm. Like he thinks it's interesting. Which makes me smile. Not an about-to-cry smile, a real smile. Then he looks at my eyes, and he's smiling too, and he's beautiful with that glow, and I *like* him. He makes me feel good. And I…I want to touch him. That's what the glow is lighting up for me: what *I* want.

I want to keep kissing him.

I want to touch more of him.

I want—*I* want—*I* want to have sex with him.

We kiss again, and fuck beer, and fuck doing what I'm supposed to, and fuck everything I've ever been taught about Be a Good Girl and Do What the Man Says. Fuck what Deanna said about sex—that it's a trade, a transaction, first he makes you feel good, then you gotta give him sex. This is what *I* want.

Maybe this is how a girl can fight. Maybe this is how a girl can win—by knowing what *she* wants, and saying yes to it.

"My mother's not home," I say to Seth. "Want to come over?"

And he smiles and he glows and he says, "Yes."

259

We're at my house. We're in my bed. He's in his boxers—he wears silk boxers—and I'm in my bra and undies. Our shoes and shirts and jeans are in the kitchen, on the stairs, in the hall. A bread crumb trail to my room.

He's lying down with his head on my pillow; I'm sitting up and digging through my nightstand junk. He tries to make me lay down with a slow, soft tug on my hair. I laugh on the outside and swoon on the in.

"Stop! St—I've gotta find my matches! I've gotta light these candles!"

He answers by tugging my hair again.

"Come *on!*" I say. "Do you have a lighter? All my matchbooks are empty."

"Nope. Don't smoke. Come here."

"Noooo! Candles! Romance! You find some good music. I'll find some matches."

I go to my dresser, run my hand through my sock drawer. My fingers find the matchbook at the same time Seth finds a station. It's that song about Spider-Man we heard a few weeks ago at the Haven.

"The Cure," Seth says.

I turn away from my dresser to look at him. It's not only his face that glows; it's his everything. His chest, smooth and tan like a stretch of Sahara, and his arms, which he's holding out like he wants to hug me. And his legs under those silk boxers. And his feet, which aren't even gross. Not even a little bit.

"The song," he says.

I turn back to my dresser, pull out the matchbook, and bring it up to my face. Sinclair's Grocery. The matches from Grant's store. From Grant's rich, safe, perfect life. The ones I said I'd never ever use.

I go back to my bed and sit down, and Seth *does* hug me. He leans up and puts his arms around my middle and his face against my back. And it's fireworks and shooting stars and lightning bolts.

"You're skin and bones," he says. "Aren't you hungry? I need to take you out for ice cream."

I'm winning. I'm a girl, and I know what I want, and I'm saying yes to it. And I'm winning.

I line the three candles up on my phone/alarm clock/radio. I flip open the Sinclair's Grocery matches, take one out, and press it to the side of the matchbook. I give it a hard push. I set it on fire.

The candles glow, and Seth glows, and I glow as I lie back into his silk-skin hug. And I win.

I'm like Tigger bouncing into English on Monday. I've been waiting all day to see Blanca, since she missed math first period because of a cheerleading meeting.

"Oh my God," I say when I see her. "I have *so* much to tell you."

Which I *so* do. I need to tell her how sweet, sweet, sweet Seth is—can you still smell his Drakkar Noir on me?!—and how he stayed at my house till he had to go to work Sunday, and how we forgot to blow out the candles, and when I finally woke up, there was all this smoke and a black circle on the ceiling and holy *fuck*, my phone/alarm clock/radio was on fire! Literally, it was melted in half! And how I'm *so* fucking lucky it didn't get to the wiring or whatever and blow *up*, and how I spent the day trying to scrub the soot off my wall and ceiling, and how Seth called me! He totally called me, and said he was *sorry* he had to leave!

I'm so stupid bouncy I don't even realize she's not looking at me until she sits down in a seat across the room. I could count every one of her curls because they're all facing me, every one of them, right there above her back.

My bouncing goes on pause, and I say, "Blanc?" but she doesn't hear me because Mrs. Skinner is saying, "Cyndy, I have a note for you from guidance." She puts it on my desk.

The note's on plain paper, not lined. It's folded in half. I'm opening it as Candy McAllister takes her seat in front of me. I'm reading it as Candy turns around. The note says,

An admissions counselor from Randolph-Macon Woman's College would like to speak with you. Please report to guidance on May 7 at 9:00 a.m.

I'm trying to process what the note means, and what Blanca's back means, as Candy leans in to me and whispers, "Cyndy, listen. You shouldn't try out for cheerleading. They're going to blackball you."

Now I know what Blanca's back is saying. It's saying I was supposed to be an outlaw. I was supposed to be *her* outlaw. Now she knows I'm more of an in-law. So now, what's my point?

The Randolph-Macon Woman's College brochures are big, shiny, and colorful. They show brick buildings, lawns criss-crossed with walkways, tulips, and trees. They show girls with friends and books and backpacks. They're paper Prozac.

"Studies show that girls participate more in all-female classes," Pam says.

Pam is the Randolph-Macon Woman's College admissions counselor. She has that sharp, blond haircut that points in at the chin, the kind that only ladies like her—with thin necks and good makeup—can pull off.

"Without the distraction of boys, the pressure of worrying about what boys think, girls gain freedom to pursue their intellectual interests."

I'm not so sure I want to be free of boys, but I open the

brochure anyway. On the inside page, there's a picture of a bedroom with a fuzzy rug and a window seat. A girl sits cross-legged on a bed. There's a book on her lap and a plate of cookies next to her. It looks like a home, like the boarding school I had thought Straight would be, before I got there and saw it was a warehouse. I make a kind of noise.

"That's one of our dorm rooms," Pam says.

"That's a dorm?" I say.

"Absolutely," Pam says with a plum-lipstick smile. "We believe that, in order for girls to work hard, they need to live soft. Our meals are served on china plates and white linen tablecloths. At Christmas, our dorm moms host tree-trimming-and-caroling-parties. Some of our dorm rooms have their own fireplace."

On the next page is a bright-green field. A girl is playing catch with a little kid as a man and lady run up to join the game.

"What's this?"

"Our Adopted Families program. We know that our out-of-town girls get homesick, so we match them up with local families who might have a child away at college themselves, or want to share their time and home with a young scholar. I have a family in mind for you, actually. The mom runs the campus day care. She would *love* you."

"And they would *adopt* me?"

Pam laughs. Her hair swings backward and forward in a perfect slice. "Well, for the school year, kind of, yes!

Anytime you get homesick, you can go over for dinner, rent movies, whatever you and your family like. We have some girls who've graduated and gone on to big careers and still come back and visit their adopted families. It's really sweet."

I rub the green of the field as I think about that. Pam and I sit quiet for a minute; then she speaks again.

"Your guidance counselor reached out to me with your name because she knew you were interested in one of the all-girls' schools in New England. It wasn't Wellesley. It was—"

"Smith."

"That's right, Smith. Forgive me if you already know this, but Smith is a *highly* selective school. They let in only a handful of their applicants. And this year, for the first time, they used financial need as a criterion. Do you know what that means?"

"If you need financial aid, you're not getting in?"

She laughs again. Like I'm funny.

"Not exactly, but it does narrow your chances. Do you know if you'll be seeking financial aid for college?"

"Oh my *God*, yes."

And again, Pam laughs. She's so pretty, even when she's laughing at me.

"Well. I don't know if your guidance counselor mentioned this, Cyndy, but I've had a chance to look over your transcripts. And while I can't put it into writing, I can all but guarantee that if you applied, you'd be welcomed at

Randolph-Macon Woman's College with open arms. And a generous aid package."

"Are you *serious*? Me?"

"I *am* serious. You."

"But *why*?"

This time when Pam laughs, she puts her hand on my arm. She's got a ring on her middle finger, heavy gold wrapped around a black onyx oval. There are tiny letters pressed into the onyx, and it looks like they spell out *Randolph-Macon Woman's College*.

"You are a firecracker, Miss Cyndy. I *like* you. I'll answer your question if you promise to keep it between us."

"Okay." It takes work, but I stop myself from pushing my finger on that onyx oval, to see if it opens a magic portal or something.

"You've heard of affirmative action?"

"Yeah…"

"Well, it's like that. We pull from the southern states, mostly—Texas, Alabama, the Carolinas. We need some Yankee girls to balance us out."

"Oh, I get it. Can I ask you a question?"

"Absolutely! You can ask me twenty!"

"Well, I really want to be a writer. Do you guys have writing classes?"

"We have a *wonderful* English program. Our English professors are famous for their round-robin Sundays. The first

Sunday of each month of the school year, an English professor hosts a dinner party for all of the English majors."

"At their *house*?!"

"At their house. Randolph-Macon Woman's is really more of a community, a family, than—"

"And where do I sign up?"

She leans her head back and does this laugh that sounds like river water. Then she goes, "Let me get you an application, Cyndy. Then you just come on down."

38

It feels weird to be in this hallway without my Dunkin' mug. It's like, a different kind of naked. But it doesn't matter because there's nobody around to stare or talk about me. The halls are fresh-waxed and empty. They only reason I'm here is because I promised Mrs. Skinner I'd come by when I was in my cap and gown. She'll see me in the procession line with everybody else, but I guess she wanted to say an actual goodbye, just to me. Which is pretty awesome, if you think about it.

Me and my mother actually stopped by Dunkin' on our way over to Masuk this morning. I wish I'd have thought to get Mrs. Skinner something. I probably would have, if I hadn't been so distracted.

On our way in, my mother goes, "We came here the morning after your last graduation too. Do you remember?"

"Yeah," I say. "After I seven stepped from Straight."

"Do you remember what I bought you that day? My gift to you?"

"Of *course*: my Dunkin' Donuts mug."

"Yes, that, and a half-dozen chocolate donuts, which you ate every *one* of."

There's a laugh behind us. Then a voice says, "Excuse me, Mrs. Etler. If you wouldn't mind, may I borrow your daughter for a moment?"

We both turn around, and my mother goes, "Cyndy, who is this charming young man?"

"I'm Doug, Mrs. Etler. Doug Bianchi."

Yes, that Doug Bianchi. Short little muscle guy. Popular kid.

"Well, *Mr.* Bianchi, you may borrow my daughter anytime you wish. Cyndy, would you like a coffee? I'll treat, since it's your graduation. Small, black, three Sweet'N Lows?"

"Yeah," I say, then turn back to see why Doug Bianchi wants to "borrow" me.

"Come on," he says, opening the door to the parking lot. Soon as we're out there he goes, "DUNK'in FOCK'in DOnuts," like it was a burp he could barely hold in.

"Yeah," I say. "Dunkin'."

"So, listen, congratulations," he says, pointing at my gown.

"Yeah, you too. Where's yours?"

"In the Rabbit. I'm not going to be seen in public in a *frock*."

270

Which makes me laugh.

"Hey, listen," Doug says. "Later. What are you doing?"

"Ummm…nothing?"

"Awesome. Want to come to a party?"

"Ummm…"

"Come on. It's graduation. You can't do *nothing*. Waddaya, a loser?"

Fuck that. "Where at?"

"Zack Fox's house."

"Zack *Fox*'s house?!" Zack Fox. Sexiest guy on the planet. Coolest kid in the school. "You sure he wants *me* there?"

"Dude, what? Of course! Zack knows you. You're *fine* with Zack. It's the *girls* you've gotta—"

The *girls*. The fucking popular girls. The cheerleaders. "Yeah, no. Thanks anyway."

"I'm *kidding*! I'm kidding. I'll pick you up. If you're with me, you'll be fine."

A house party. At a kid like Zack Fox's house. On the night of my graduation. That's the ultimate mega-dream come true. It's also the ultimate mega-threat to my sobriety. Because what do you *do* at a house party, other than drink and drug? Like, work on math problems?

But it's my fucking graduation. I mean, I *did* this. I *got* here. I stayed *alive*. So maybe fuck what I'm supposed to do. Maybe fuck being a Straightling. Maybe fuck playing by the rules.

This is how a girl can win—by knowing what she wants, and saying yes to it.

"Okay, yeah."

"Awesome! I'll see you at three o'clock. Wear a bathing suit."

And, fuck. A bathing suit?! No wonder I didn't think to get Mrs. Skinner anything from fucking Dunkin'.

"Hi, Mrs. Skinner," I say when I walk into her room. She looks up from her grade book. She has on frosty pink lipstick. There's a flower behind her ear.

"Cyndy, look at you!" she says.

She comes around her desk and gives me a real hug. When she pulls back, she keeps her hands on my shoulders and looks me in the eyes.

"Some people need makeup to be beautiful," she says. "You are one of those rarities who do not. You are beautiful, and you are wise. Now. Go out into the world and write."

She hands me a purple envelope and turns away, blowing her nose into a hanky.

I open the envelope as I'm walking out of her room. The card inside is a painting of a girl on a rock. She's got craggy red cliffs behind her and swirling purple clouds above. Her dress is blowing back and her hands are in her hair, and she's looking upward with a private kind of smile. Inside the card it says, "You are going to be fine. In fact, you already are. Love, Polly Skinner."

I slide the card back into its envelope and look up to check the big clock in the main office. But I can't see it because the main office window is covered with stars. Cut-out paper stars. With people's names on them.

"Our Graduating Superstars!" it says above the window in glitter letters. The names are arranged randomly, not alphabetically, because Tiffani Malta's name is up on the left, and there's Zack Fox's, all the way at the bottom. Jack Pilgrim is right in the middle. Somebody drew a skull and crossbones on his. I hope I'm not late for graduation, but fuck it. Even though Deanna doesn't call me anymore, she's the best sober friend I'll ever have. I've gotta find her star. I've gotta bring her with me.

I'm looking and looking—the stars are all jumbling together, and I'm starting to think about pulling the not-Dee stars off the window, to speed up my search—when it hits me. Deanna doesn't have a star. She's not graduating. She dropped out.

For some reason, that feels like the saddest thing ever. It feels like a penny dropped from a skyscraper. Some people don't make it.

But I did. I've got a star up there.

I start searching again, for my star this time. And there it is, way up near the top. My name is spelled right, in black Magic Marker:

CYNDY ETLER

Right above my name, in pencil, somebody graffitied something. I step closer and squinch my eyes to make it out. It looks like a heart. I'm pretty sure it says—yeah, it does. That's what it says.

I ♥
CYNDY ETLER

I'm sitting on the roof next to Doug Bianchi. Zack Fox is up here with us, on the other side of Doug. Doug's talking wicked fast about some rude thing his brother did and how he's gonna join the marines and show his brother, who's only in the navy.

"ShaddAP, Dougie," yells Ty.

I can't believe Ty talked. Legends don't talk. They do shit like float around the pool in a Styrofoam armchair, with their eyes closed and their paw gripping an uncracked beer. Doug, the un-legend, keeps yammering.

"Jeezus, kid. What're you, on coke?" Ty yells, which makes Zack laugh, and Brent laugh, and Doug turn bright, bright red. I kinda laugh too, even though I'm not supposed to. I mean, without Doug, I wouldn't be within a trillion miles of this place.

I'm here, though. At a popular party. Laughing at a joke about cocaine. If the people at Straight could see me now, I'd be on the firing line. Three hundred Straightlings would be gearing up to spit on me, screeching, *Sobriety! Slippery slope!*

But maybe...maybe I'm not a Straightling anymore. Maybe I'm something else. Maybe I'm just a kid, like everyone at the Haven, like everyone who graduated Masuk today. Maybe I'm not a fuckup or a druggie or a whore. Maybe I'm just another kid.

I hear the crack of the opening can at the same second Brent starts yelling. It sounds like the crack of a—

"Doug! Douggieee! Jump, Dougie! Jump!"

Brent's splashing in the shallow end, curling his arms, to show Doug the path from roof to pool. There's another crack, and Zack passes Doug one of the beers he must have had in his Levi's back pockets. That's twice today that beer has been within three feet of me. And I laughed at a cocaine joke.

What even is cocaine, though? Seriously. I've never seen it. I've never touched it. But I'm shitting my pants thinking about it, like a little kid with the boogeyman under his bed. We were forced to admit we were addicts in Straight. And then we were forced to believe it. But, really, was I? Addicted? I never wanted drugs or alcohol. What I wanted was the friends that came with them. I wanted to escape my mother's husband. I wanted to not be alone.

And look. I'm not alone. I'm here, at this popular-kid party. *I* did this. *I* got here.

"Dougie baby! Come to mama!" goes Brent.

"Here," Doug says, shoving his—his *beer* into my hand.

I hold it by two fingers like it burns. "Wait, I—"

Wait. I don't have to freak out. I had beer in my *mouth* that night at the Haven, when Seth took a sip and then kissed me. In my *mouth*. It didn't make me run out and pick up the first joint I saw. It didn't make me snort coke off the floor of a truck stop men's room. All it did was make me sip soda, to swish the nasty beer taste out of my mouth.

"Go ahead," Doug says. "Take a sip."

"Do it, Cyn," Zack says.

"Douggieee!" Brent yells.

"Doug-ie! Doug-ie!" says Ty and the popular girls, through the cotton of the tank tops they're pulling over their heads.

"You take a sip, and I jump," Doug says to me.

Which should be terrifying, but it isn't. Because it's not beer that has power over me. Or drugs. Or my mother's ex-husband. Or Straight. It's me. I've got the power. To tell my mother to take me to the psychiatrist. To bring Seth back to my house. To stay alive.

A car is pulling up outside Zack Fox's house. Windows

down, stereo cranked. It's so loud I can feel the rumble of the base. The song is one of the Club 12 party starters, where everybody crammed onto the dance floor. We'd all sing the lyrics, loud, because the song told the whole story. There *is* joy. There *is* pain. And then the sun shines, and then there's rain. It all comes and goes. And you just…*handle* it.

Doug's right at the edge of the roof. He's staring at me and shaking his fists up and down, like a baby banging on its tray.

The elite-level popular kids are all going, "Doug-ie! Doug-ie!"

"One sip," Doug says, "and I jump. Ready, set, *go*."

"Sunshine! R—" The car clicks off.

I put my lips on the beer.

I tip it back.

Doug jumps off the roof.

And the world explodes in cheers and splashing water.

A NOTE FROM THE AUTHOR

So about that sex thing.

I know there are people who wait for true love. That's some powerful shit.

Then there are people who can't wait another *second* for love. That's some *real* shit.

If you're like me—if you've been scraping and searching every day of your life to try to feel close to somebody—sex can seem like a decent trade for love. If you don't feel cherished at home, if you don't have a true group of friends, if you don't have a place you just *belong*, sex can look like the safe, sweet everything you've always wanted.

Movies, ads, books, that frigging couple holding hands in the hallway—they all make it look like everybody has someone who loves them. Everybody but *you*. So when a cute guy or girl shows up and shows interest? Boom. You jump into taking off your clothes. Because finally *you* are gonna have love too.

And maybe you will—for like a minute. Maybe even five. People can be very persuasive, very flattering, when they have a goal. When that goal is *you*, well God *damn*, does that attention feel good. So maybe you roll with it. If you read this book, you know I did. But afterward, when the attention was gone and the boy was too? *Man.* That kind of alone was worse than anything, because it felt so much more personal. Like he actually knew me and *then* decided he didn't like me.

It is totally not my objective to convince you to do, or not do, anything.[1] But I would like to share what I've learned about how sex works, some stuff I don't hear anyone else talking about. Maybe, if my ideas makes sense, you won't have to deal with the pain that I did. Okay, so.

Remember Connie, who taught me I had to "kill my babies" to make my writing good? She also taught me this ancient wisdom about gender roles: "Men want. Women want to be wanted." Like the *best* thing that can happen,

---

1. Except when it comes to using protection. Birth control pill, dental dam, condom, whatever: if you *do* decide to have sex, make sure you've got what you need to be safe. And be ready to be that badass who, when things get going, says, "Hey, listen, we're gonna use this."

for a lot of guys, is to get sex. And the best thing that can happen, for lots of girls, is to get attention.

I know you're like, "That's so stupid!" But hold up. If that's so stupid, why do so many girls work so hard to look Kardashian-sexy? If that's so stupid, why are so many teen girls sending nude pictures of themselves to boys? Because *still*—I puke as I type this, but *still*—a girl's value is in her sexiness. To feel valuable, girls make themselves look sexy.

But here's another ancient truth that doesn't get a lot of media attention: *girls have pleasure receptors too*. We all know boys enjoy sex stuff...but girls can too. Crazy, right?! The female body is built to feel pleasure, the same way the male body is. That pleasure just gets blocked by the brain, by the antique message that's still kicking around, telling girls "your job is to look good and keep your legs closed."

So. If you're a girl, or if you're a boy, there are probably things you'd like to do, and things you would *not* like to do, and things you won't *know* if you want to do, until you try them. How about if you think about those things now, on your own, before you're in a heated situation? If you know what you're cool with ahead of time, in the moment it's a simple yes or no. But if you don't know what your basic yeses and nos are ahead of time, it's tempting to roll with what the other person is suggesting...even if it's good for *them,* but not for you.

When you're in that heated situation, you can say no.

And the other person might walk away. Also, you can say yes. And the other person *still* might walk away. Sometimes people use people for sex. For ego pump. For whatever the fuck. And then they ditch. And that shit *hurts*. But then… the hurt stops. Promise. When you find something else that lights up your brain, it stops hurting. The trick is knowing how to find that thing that will light your brain up.

Hint: Trying to get that person's attention back will not light up your brain. It will slice up your soul. Seriously. If I had gone back to Grant's store, would he have suddenly wanted to take me out on dates? Duh. How about if I had returned to Club 12 to ask Damien, again, if he wanted to go skating with me? Would he have changed his mind? No chance. It's obvious in my story. It will work the same way in yours. Trust me. Find. Something. Kinder.

Here's how: ask yourself another question. Try to really listen and be open to your own answers. The Q: What do your mind and body really want?

Physical closeness that involves sex stuff? With what gender? How far do you want to go?

Physical closeness that's just affectionate and huggy?

Romance-y stuff, like dates? What would be fun to do? Can you do those things even if you don't have a girlfriend/boyfriend? Who with? If you don't have friends who are down to do this kind of stuff, would it be fun to do them on your own? (Seriously. Consider the idea of "dating yourself."

I *know*, but the longer you think about it, the better it sounds. Who wants to do what you want to do more than *you*? Plus, when you start to enjoy your own company, you no longer want to waste your time on people who aren't as cool/kind/ interesting as you are.)

A feeling of social belonging, of closeness with others? Are there ways to find that feeling other than sex?

Hint: Yup, there really are. Promise. You'll find where you belong faster if you can ID what *you* are really into—for me, it's writing, dogs, and being in the woods—and look for those who love the same stuff. If you're social, find groups at school that are doing whatever you're interested in. If you're more comfortable behind a screen, search out online groups that are discussing whatever you're interested in:

- book/writing/anime/gaming/activism/what- ever clubs at the library or online
- church youth groups
- Boys and Girls' Clubs, or scouting, or local community center groups
- ask your neighbors if you can walk their dog. And take that dog hiking in the woods. You'll never find a better friend than a dog, and you'll never find more calm *good* than you will in the woods. Swear to God.

And back to the sex: if you were abused as a child, you may have absorbed the lesson that "This is all you're good for; you have to do this stuff whenever somebody wants you to."[2] If that mess sounds familiar, let me be the first to tell you: That is some *bull*shit. That is somebody else's control drama. You can just shake that shit off now, like a scungy, hand-me-down overcoat. When you were little, maybe somebody else told you what coat you had to wear. Maybe you didn't know you could say no. But now, you can see how icky that thing is. Just take it off. Burn it. Choose a new coat. Choose whatever coat *you* want to wear.

We had to sing a lot of crappy songs in Straight. Probably the crappiest was Whitney Houston's "The Greatest Love of All." The punch line was that the greatest love of all was loving her*self*. I know. Talk about puke. But seriously. When you start respecting yourself—by knowing what *you* like and doing what *you* feel comfortable with—people sense it, and start treating you better. Weirdly, they start liking you more.

So. Maybe life sucks right now. Maybe it hurts. Maybe you feel totally alone. But you're not. You've got *you*. And if

---

2. If you were abused as a child, or are being abused, there are tons of resources and people who can help you deal with it. Who can help you *get* safe, if you're not safe right now, and help you *feel* safe, if the abuse was in the past.

   Asking for help isn't easy. It can be scary and awkward. There's a good chance you may not feel like you deserve help, because you've been told you're "making it up," you're "just trying to get attention," or some other victim-blamey line that abusers use to keep you silent. But baby, listen to me: if you feel like you have been abused, that's all you need to know. Trust yourself.

you're like me, once it hits you that you actually like *yourself* better than you like anybody else? Well, shit. Suddenly the whole world's lining up to love you. Swear to God.

To find help, look for an adult who seems interested in you, without wanting anything for themselves. In addition to guidance counselors, there are cool, caring adults in many other roles that work with youth: librarians, teachers, nurses, LGTBQ-club mentors, that friend's parent who actually *looks* at you when they ask how you're doing... Of course, you can also find help through organizations, many of which are also online: BornThisWay. Foundation, LoveIsRespect.org, and PlannedParenthood.org are just a few of the many good ones.

To start the conversation, you can keep it really simple. When you say, text, or hand a kind adult a slip of paper that says "I don't feel safe," you're taking the first step to *getting* safe. It might be the first of many steps, but you can get here, I swear. Safety is possible. I know, because I live in it. Finally. Come join me.

ACKNOWLEDGMENTS

Since I could move a crayon across paper, I wanted to be a writer. More than I wanted a boyfriend. More than I wanted a family. More than I wanted designer jeans, even. I wanted to be a writer. When I was writing, and again when I was editing (and editing and editing), the scenes in this book where people said they liked my writing, I cried with gratitude and shock. Because it started way back then, and it's happening now. My sharp, shining, impossible dream is coming true. You're holding it in your hand. I'm—I'm a real, true writer.

To all you fairy godmothers who sprinkled magic on the process, who saw glint in my words and *told* me so, I thank you. I thank you. I thank you: Ellen Hopkins. Myrsini Stephanides. Annette Pollert-Morgan. Penny O'Dell. Jane

Cochran. LouAnne Johnson. Mercy Pilkington. Rachel Rubin. Nancy Noonan. Connie from CoDa. And you hundreds of students and cohorts and readers and writers in classes and workshops and writing groups who said to me, "Damn. You can *write*. Keep writing."

And to you former kids who were cool with me when I was weird, thank you. Thank you, Christina. Shawn. Maryann. Tim. Gina. Senya. Dave. Heather. Shelby. Diana. Steve.

And to you Sourcebooks pros who roll with my comma obsession, who answer my zillion questions, who make these books lush and important and gorgeous, thank you. Thank you: Alex Yeadon. Heather Moore. Cassie Gutman. Gretchen Stelter. Sarah Kasman. Dominique Raccah.

And to you pagan angels who give me love and safety, thank you. Thank you. I love you. Eric. Eli. Oscar.

ABOUT THE AUTHOR

A modern-day Cinderella, Cyndy Etler was homeless at thir-teen and *summa cum laude* at thirty. As a teacher and teen life coach, she convinces kids that books work better than drugs. She lives with her brilliant husband and adorable rescue dogs in North Carolina. Find her at cyndyetler.com.